P T K

PARENTS
TEACHERS
KIDS

PARENTS
TEACHERS
KIDS

By
Wm. R. Van Osdol, Ph.D.
Central State University

MSS INFORMATION CORPORATION

Distributed by **ARNO PRESS**
3 Park Avenue, New York, N.Y. 10016

Library of Congress Cataloging in Publication Data

Van Osdol, William R
   P. T. K.; Parents Teachers Kids

   1. Child psychiatry. 2. Parent and child.
3. Teacher-student relationships. I. Title.
II. Title: Parents Teachers Kids
RJ499.V36   371.9'01'9   74-6352
ISBN 0-8422-5167-7
ISBN 0-8422-0395-8 (pbk.)

CONTENTS

SECTION ONE

Emotionally Disturbed and
Behaviorally Maladjusted Children

SECTION TWO

Psychological Behavior

SECTION THREE
Intellectual Behavior

SECTION FOUR
Influential Behavior

TABLES

Preface

P. T. K. contains a number of dialogues which concern adult-child interpersonal relationships. These dialogues are in alphabetical order, by section, and one dialogue is not to be considered more important than another. The reader does not have to begin reading on page one and read continuously. Each dialogue may be read in any preferred order. Some of the dialogues are supported by references and research relative to specific behaviors and treatment of behavior. Other dialogues simply relate some very basic adult-child considerations for good emotional growth. The dialogues are written in the first person, and as the author I will refer to my experiences, beliefs, and suggestions. All concepts of human behavior, naturally, cannot be comprehensive in one book, but P. T. K. will allow the readers enough information to enable them to have an awareness of emotional behavior that is manifested among and between adults and children. The awareness of behavior should, then, reflect the power with which personal interactions affect the home, school, and/or person.

The book is divided into four sections, Section One, gives a general baseline for understanding emotionally disturbed children and the effects that maladjusted behavior may have on the home, school, teachers, parents and children.

Section two is concerned with the more serious psychological pathologies of behavior, and offers a guide to understanding these symptoms as they may exist within one's environment.

Section three offers information relative to intellectual behaviors. This section is short and covers only three areas of learning, and is by no means a complete guide for procedural contact, but does offer guidelines toward understanding the emotional growth process of the gifted, the learning disabled, and mentally retarded children.

Section four consists of a large number of short dialogues on different kinds of behavior that have considerable influence upon other behaviors and upon life. These dialogues offer many specific "common sense" kinds of suggestions for adult-child interpersonal interaction; and I believe each reader could profit by his reading and practicing these behavioral suggestions.

Wm. R. Van Osdol

SECTION ONE

EMOTIONALLY DISTURBED
AND BEHAVIORALLY
MALADJUSTED CHILDREN

EMOTIONALLY DISTURBED

A N D

BEHAVIORALLY MALADJUSTED CHILDREN

Introduction

I should like to discuss somewhat generally the characteristics and symptoms that are visible to parents and teachers of disturbed children, a n d s o m e suggested practices for child-adult interaction. It is impossible to offer a clear-cut definition, but a number of symptoms o r characteristics do exist that a r e generally included within a disturbed child's behavioral framework.   Disturbed children have worries, anxieties, and other generalized fears within themselves, which i n turn cause them t o behave in a somewhat inaffective manner at home and at school. Therefore, teachers and parents should be alerted to these signs and symptoms.

Many times kids will translate their fears a n d anxieties into physical symptoms. They seem to have frequent physical complaints, and worry considerably about their health. These children may malinger and hold onto their illnesses to the point of being able t o find excuses for inner tension in some physical difficulty. These children also seem t o have numerous accidents. They frequently w i l l have cuts, scratches, broken bones, etc.

Another child may attempt to solve his anxiety by going back to or regressing to earlier forms of behavior. T h i s regression will give him security because he knows how to deal with problems at an immature level. Regression happens t o all o f us a t t i m e s when we meet frustrating situations that we can't handle. Consequently we will return to a form of behavior that is comfortable for us.

Another child may indicate his fears and anxieties through aggressive a c t s toward other people-- parents, teachers or friends. In effect, he tries to overcome his anxieties by taking things into his own hands. He is, of course, unable t o cope with his problems through aggression, and only confirms the fact that he is a problem riddled child. Aggression has recently been increasing, but there is no particular evidence for the increase. Television, movies, and less structure are possible contributions, but nothing empirical has been indicated. It is interesting to note, though, that a significant increase in aggressive acts h a v e been indicated by elementary school age children.

Children may, instead o f becoming aggressive, withdraw into fantasy land. Teachers and parents call these children daydreamers; because the children do not relate well to their peers or to adults, and become isolated in the classrooms.

Some disturbed children fear failure and criticism; and therefore, become perfectionists. Everything has to be just right, and when stimuli or behavior are not compatible with his world, he is in a turmoil.

Other children may avoid real anxieties by developing substitute fears, compulsions, and phobias. To these phobias they attach emotional reactions which interfere with their overall functioning.

Any of the conditions about which we've just mentioned may produce poor social and school adjustment. As a general rule, though, one must realize that poor school and social adjustment are not always the result of emotional disturbances.

It is generally felt that the teachers have considerable sensitivity and insight into the problem behavior of disturbed children. Yes, I realize this is not true in all teaching situations, but most teachers do recognize the obvious deviations of problem-plagued children; and it is the conduct problem child who has the liability for possibly creating severe emotional disturbances in his adult life. Therefore, it is not unusual for other disciplines to look to the schools for help in reducing the rate of psychological mental health problems.

Teachers and school personnel are important links to a multi-disciplinary approach to mental health. Emotional disturbance is not the result of a suddenly developed condition, but it is a development that emits visible cues and is sometimes susceptible to evaluation early in a child's life; therefore, a teacher who spends a great number of hours with a child is able to observe that disturbed children generally score significantly lower on group I.Q. tests, on reading and arithmetic tests, and that they differ from other children in self-perception as indicated by test items on personality inventories.

These teachers may also observe that disturbed boys generally exhibit greater dissatisfaction with themselves and their school behavior than other boys and that disturbed girls exhibit less dissatisfaction with themselves than other girls in the class. Also on sociograms other children in the classes have a tendency to select disturbed children as the trouble makers in the class. Therefore, it appears that even other children can judge quite accurately the disturbed child's behavior as a personality that is unwholesome for general classroom activities.

Teachers, also, can observe that the disturbed child's problems increase with each grade level. As the child is moved to a higher grade his problems become more severe. He is faced with the increased successful aspirations of other children and his own inability to function at the higher level. In essence, the successful child is more successful and the failing child is meeting more failure. The teacher may additionally realize that some disturbed children perform well in academic work, but their behavior may bother the teacher and the other children, and retard the total objectives or goals of the class.

The good teacher will recognize that there is something about the child or his behavior that causes her to feel anxiety and frustration toward the child. Consequently, the disturbed child has a feeling of personal discomfort in a school classroom. This discomfort may cause the child to withdraw or drop out of the class or school completely. Therefore, school problems as reported by parents and teachers are associated with the expectations of parents, teachers, and children. The total of a teacher's observation of children's behavior, then, should be indicative of the awareness that teachers have to problem-oriented children; and the teacher's observations and assessments should be fairly well in line with the testing observations of a clinician--psychologist, social worker, psychiatrist, etc. In other words, teachers, don't sell yourselves short, because you contribute a great deal to the child's good mental health.

Emotional disturbance may be characterized by withdrawal or an alienation from school, but there also may be behavioral traits which are categorized as subcultural or socialized delinquency. Therefore, the educational disability may be a symptom of the condition (cultural or social) which produces the emotional problems rather than being caused by the emotional problems.

There seems to be observational evidence which indicates that arithmetic disability is associated with severe personality problems whereas reading disability is simply because the child is behind in the grade placement. I am not saying, though, that personality disorders per se are the only cause for arithmetic problems. Some of these children will have total academic failure, and it should not be indicated that only severe personality maladjustment is the cause. I've also seen children who are severly disturbed, but they do not have academic problems. Generally, though, the children who are disturbed will have school problems.

We should be careful not to label children as emotionally disturbed simply because they do not fall under the qubric of some other exceptionality, and

are unable to adjust to the regular school classroom .
Consequently, we should b e aware that a child's inability to adjust to a regular class i s n o t adequate
assessment for classification as disturbed.   T h e r e
are certain symptoms o r behaviors which can be measured by their frequency, tenure, and severity, which
tend to categorize themselves into t w o major areas--
acting out behavior (conduct problems), a n d withdrawn behavior (personality disorders).

Definition

Many theories of personality, child behavior, and
remediation presently exist within the framework of
the emotionally or behaviorally disturbed child. M y
personal experiences have indicated t h a t it is extremely difficult to find a perfect definition f o r
the disturbed child. A definition must b e   relevant
t o the many different cultures, societies, and moral
values.   A n y single definition doesn't s e e m to be
consistent w i t h the needs of all professionals o r
theories of treatment.

Kessler (1966) has indicated the following guidelines as referral criteria for disturbed children:
1. Age discrepancy.   There a r e ages by which
    most children have outgrown particular hab-
    its and behavior.
2. Frequency of occurrence o f the symptom must
    be considered. One should be concerned when
    the symptomatic behavior is aroused   under
    minimal stress, which means it occurs very
    often.
3. The number of symptoms is a n obvious consi-
    deration. The more symptoms, the more t h e

17

child is disabled. However, one should not rely exclusively on the criterion of multiplicity of symptoms to judge the extent of psychopathology. It is possible for a single symptom to work so efficiently that all the child's anxieties are taken care of at once. All of his problems may be bound up in the one phobic situation so that there is no spillage into other areas.

4. The degree of social disadvantage is an inevitable determinant of parental concern about the children's symptoms. It is easy to see a vicious circle at work where the effects of symptom may tend to perpetuate the symptom.

5. The child's inner suffering is often overlooked. It is often assumed that the child's opinion of himself is based solely on the spoken statement of others. So, if the parents are tolerant, and outsiders do not know about the symptom, the parents may feel that the child will not be upset about it. But children are quite capable of judging themselves. And though he may not verbalize his inner distress, he often reveals it to someone who knows him well.

6. Intractability of behavior is implied, in part, in the criterion of frequency. The persistence of symptoms, despite the efforts of the child and others to change them, is the hallmark of so-called behavior disorders.

7. General personality appraisal is the most important criterion, and the most difficult.

18

This criterion has to do with the child's general adjustment, rather than isolated symptoms.

Before one is able to describe abnormal or different behavior, one should have some workable concepts of normal behavior. If one were to describe normal behavior, a judgement must be made concerning one's own values, his immediate environment's values, and live in a static world today. Their environment and cultures are constantly changing, and the children must learn to switch from one role of behavior to a different role. Behavior and values which are acceptable in one school or city may not be tolerated in another school. Values of the child's home or community may not be acceptable in his school; therefore, this child must learn early in life that he will have to play many different roles of behavior.

Apparently one of the most serious concerns for behavior deviations is that which prevents a child from maintaining a normal pattern of intellectual, social, and emotional growth in the public schools. Schools have achievement records and tests which supposedly determine normal ranges of progress for various academic subjects. Therefore, certain expectations exist for children within particular age ranges. Rubin, Simson, and Betwee (1966), indicate that children can be identified as failing to make appropriate and significant progress in certain well established and accepted areas of accomplishment, such as at school. They also feel that necessary patterns of adaptation for any given age period may be defined, and deviance from these may be a useful guide to the identification of maladaptation.

Many definitions of disturbed behavior appear to center around the child's inability to maintain himself adequately in the home, school, and community. Buhier, Smitter, and Richardson (1966) have indicated that in psychological terms, a problem is a hindrance that may disrupt the continuity of the processes within an individual or a group. An example would be a child's problem in school which disrupts the classwork, the desirable cooperation of the group, and/or the child's own ability to function.

Kessler (1966) writes that the criteria for judging a child's need for help should be considerate of three behaviors--progression, fixation, and regression. I am in agreement with Kessler's view that a child is growing, changing, and developing, and as a consequence of this interaction with his world his behavior is constantly changing. The changes in behavior, though, may be indicated by either a static display, which in affect will cause the child to regress because he cannot maintain proper peer relations if he does not move forward; or he actually may manifest serious regressions, which will result in a significant lag in growth; or he will move forward toward maturity and acceptable growth. Hopefully, of course, all children will move forward in an acceptable way of life. Realistically, though, one must realize that some children will manifest behaviors that cannot be tolerated in their schools, homes, and communities.

One must always be aware that some children can succeed in one or more areas (e.g., school) of life, but may be completely debilitated in another area (e.g., home or neighborhood). Therefore, the child's total level of functioning must be considered when determining a definition of a disturbed child. Consequently, my experiences have indicated that a definition for an emotionally and/or behaviorally disturbed child must reflect a child's inability to function compatibly with the total environment in which he must live. A definition which appears to encompass these environments would be one which defines the emotionally disturbed child as a child who cannot emotionally, intellectually, and socially function in a manner that is acceptable by his peers, teachers, parents, and legal authorities within his school, home, and community environment.

Early detection can be dangerous because without treatment, early detection can lead to a self-fulfilling prophesy. Also, by alerting parents or teachers to possible future difficulties, their anxieties are increased, which will reduce their effectiveness unless they are given some directions. Therefore, without any promise of treatment, early diagnosis may only compound the problem and prove to be a curse in disguise.

Methods of identification must be consistent with the knowledge that is available from the many different areas of human behavior. A teacher, psychologist, social worker, psychiatrist, child development specialist, or guidance counselor is not equipped to make a conclusive report upon a child's emotional problems. Each person, who is concerned with this child's emotional health, should be a contributing member of a team that suggests methods of identification and treatment. I have witnessed singular diagnosis of children that were blatantly in error, and these errors of judgement became visible only after there had been an evaluation review from a composite of different professional personnel. Evidence in theory and practice does not support the fact that one person has the singular professional skill to determine the life course of a particular child. Therefore, assistance from another p e r s o n who m a y know something about t h e child's school, home, or community skills m a y be of great importance in determining whether a child is to be tested or treated for emotional disturbances.

Characteristics of emotional disturbances are so plentiful that one would have difficulty in trying to tabulate all of them. Apparently, though, each behavioral scientist has his specific method of coding t h e s e children into distinct areas of behavior or disturbances. I will list an overview of some of the current practices of characterizing disturbed children and hope that the reader will not conclude that it is an easy process t o separate t h e disturbed from the non-disturbed c h i l d when both children possess the same or similar characteristics.

Chapman (1965) reports that psychoneurosis designates a group of emotional disorders in children which may be divided into different categories of behavior:

1. Phobias, which are abnormal fears of specific things or situations. Phobias constitute the most common psychoneurotic disturbance o f childhood.

2. Anxiety Reactions, in which the child experiences much tension, varying from mild restlesness to sheer panic; they may be acute or chronic.

3. Obsessive and Compulsive Reactions, in obsessive reactions the patient is afflicted with

persistent, distressing i d e a s of which he cannot r i d himself, and i n the compulsive s t a t e s he feels strong urges t o perform repeated physical acts t o relieve tension.

4. Conversion and Dissociative Reactions, which include various disorders of sensation, movement, and spatial sensory perception. The term conversion reaction is, in general, synonymous with the older term hysteria . The dissociative disorders a r e clinically related and are more characterized by disturbances of awareness or memory, as in psychogenic amnesias.

5. Tics, which are discrete, repetitive, muscular movements, are caused by emotional t e nsion. Because m i l d tics a r e common i n children and have particular characteristics, we shall treat them as a separate category, though tics in adults are often i n c l u d ed under the conversion reactions.

Many symptoms may be characteristic of "normal" behavior, and these symptoms, even though present, do not cause any functional problems within one's environment. The same symptoms exhibited within a disturbed child's repertoire may cause considerable distracted behavior. Such things as nail-biting to the "normal" child may not become an obstacle, but to the disturbed child this type o f symptom may b e the overlay of a very serious problem. Each nail-biting session is then a very anxiety provoking situation. Some disturbed children will n o t manifest characteristics such as bed-wetting, nail-biting, or thumbsucking as distinct symptoms of anxious behavior. T h e y will, instead, invest themselves into a personality structure that causes difficulties in their total interpersonal relationships. Chapman (1965) had divided what he refers to as interpersonal and personality functioning behavior into three general areas:

1. Personality -- pattern disturbances, in which the emotional troubles of the child produce problems in his personality structure. This category includes the depressed child, the passive child, the aggressive child, and the emotionally insecure child.

2. Acting-out behavior disorders, in which the child acts out hostile feelings in anti-social ways. Examples are running away, use of alcohol and illicit drugs, stealing, lying, school truancy, and fire-setting.

3. Disorders of sexual behavior, in which emotional turmoil produces disturbances of sexual behavior, or in homosexuality, and transvestism.

Disorders of the learning and training processes of children may cause maladjustment in the acquisition of the necessary skills for communication, social, and academic proficiency. Children are somewhat characterized by their experiential framework. Therefore, if the child's world has been infested with socially inappropriate behaviors he will probably gravitate to these behaviors and appear to be a helpless, paralyzed, dependent, non-communicative child. Chapman, (1965) has approached a three-section division of disorders in training, learning, and speech as possible characteristics of emotionally disturbed children:

1. Adjustment disorders of habit training, in which a socially necessary type of training is not developed, as in enuresis and encopresis. This group also includes thumbsucking, hair-pulling, and sleep disturbances.
2. Adjustment disorders of l e a r n i n g , which include difficulties in mastering the skill of scholastic learning, all of which involve the use of symbols. Examples a r e , reading problems and general learning inhibitions.
3. Adjustment disorders of speech, which include delayed speech, stuttering, a n d disorders of speech articulation.

Chapman also divides psychosomatic illnesses into categories characteristic of some emotionally disturbed children. I contend that there really isn't much need to sort out the psychosomatic illnesses into distinct areas of illnesses, because the concern should not be for a child's specific malingering illness, but concern should be for the fact t h a t he is ill. T h e specific k i n d of illness manifested-- asthma, ulcers, hyperventilation, acne, headaches, abdominal pains, chest pains, back aches, etc.--are n o t as important characteristically as i s the fact that the child consistently manifests these illnesses and symptoms, when no apparent organistic cause c a n be determined. The physician will quite likely impress medical treatment u p o n the child in the same manner as he would with other children. It is interesting to note, though, that disturbed children will manifest varying kinds and degrees of severity of the psychosomatic illnesses, a n d placebo o r medication application will have relatively little effect upon his aches and pains for any significant period of time. Therefore, one should note the frequency and tenure of the child's illness and the child's response to his illness.

Many characteristics of emotionally disturbed children should be evident to the classroom teacher. These characteristics may clearly present obstacles before the child's progress or they may remain somewhat subtle. The teacher is exposed to the child for the second largest number of hours in each day, and the child probably is in a position at school to exhibit his problems even more obviously than he would in many home situations. Therefore, a considerable number of different kinds of characteristics of behavior should be visible to the teacher. Bower (1969) has indicated five different areas from which a teacher could observe visible signs of trouble:

1. An inability to learn which cannot be explained by intellectual, sensory, or health factors.
2. An inability to build or maintain satisfactory interpersonal relationships with peers and teachers.
3. Inappropriate types of behavior or feelings under normal conditions.
4. A general, pervasive mood of unhappiness or depressions.
5. A tendency to develop physical symptoms, pains, or fears associated with personal or school problems.

In a study conducted in California, Bower (1969) noted that the emotionally disturbed child differed

26

from other c h i l d r e n in the following ways: He
scored significantly lower on group I. Q. tests.   He
scored significantly lower on reading and arithmetic
achievement tests.   Other children tended to select
him for hostile, inadequate, or negative, rather than
positive roles in class activities.

Quay, Morse and Cutler (1966) s u b j e c t e d the
Peterson Problem Behavior Rating Scale t o   a   factor
a n a l y s i s on a variety o f populations, and these
studies indicated that three independent dimensions
account for about two-thirds of t h e variance of the
interrelationships among problem behaviors.   T h e s e
three dimensions, of course, possess activity that may
be characteristic of emotionally disturbed children.
The first dimension listed aggressive, hostile a n d
contentious behaviors , which a r e also referred to as
c o n d u c t disorders, unsocialized aggressions,   or
psychopathologies. The second dimension included the
anxious, withdrawn, introvertive kinds o f behavior,
which also have been labeled personality problem or
neuroticism.   The third dimension considered preoccupation, lack of interest,   sluggishness, laziness,
daydreaming, a n d passivity.   T h e third   dimension
generally seems t o have accounted for much less o f
a variance than the first two dimensions.

Children's strange behaviors are many times the
e m i s s i o n of and hopefully the detection of their
problems. The child will express himself   possibly
in many different avenues o f behavior a n d h e will
undoubtedly defense his actions as being acceptable.
Unknown t o himself, and many times to those   around
him, the child is expressing a need for help through

his unacceptable behavior. Morse (1969) points out the importance of being able to detect the symptoms of the emotionally disturbed child. His reasoning is that most disturbed children are still in regular classrooms, and probably will continue to be there until more and better provisions are made for them. Therefore, he sees the need for the teacher to be able to recognize a child's symptoms which indicate that he is having a problem, and is calling for help.

If teachers and professionals are able to discover the cry for help from a disturbed child; they should consider many questions relevant to a particular child's behavior and background. It should be noted, though, that a child does not necessarily emit all the characteristics that are listed below. These different behaviors are possible characteristics possessed in large numbers by some whildren, and possessed in small quantities by others. I have had experiences with a number of disturbed children, who emitted excessive unacceptable behavior through expression of the different characteristics that are listed below: This list of characteristics is not conclusive but it does contain a number of important considerations for those who are concerned about identifying emotionally disturbed children:

1. Does the child express excessive anger?
2. Does the child appear hostile?
3. Does the child have significant academic deficiencies?
4. Does the child appear to maintain acceptable physical hygiene?
5. Does he appear to receive adequate sleep?
6. Is he sleepy and bored with school?

7. Does he appear negative?
8. Is he exceptionally hyperactive?
9. Is he significantly withdrawn from his peers?
10. Does his I. Q. score appear to be compatible with his functioning level?
11. Does he participate in extracurricular activities
12. Is he destructive to property?
13. Does he have temper tantrums in school or at home?
14. Is he truant or tardy consistently?
15. Does he appear to be depressed or exhibit suicidal tendencies?
16. Is he suspicious of the teacher and his peers?
17. Does he appear to have hallucinations or delusions?
18. Does he complain of physical illnesses?
19. Do his moods vascillate from pleasant to unpleasant?
20. Is there indication of sexual preoccupation?
21. Is there indication of stealing, fire-setting, or enuretic behavior?
22. Does he exhibit sudden emotional outbursts?
23. Is his self-image depreciatory?
24. Is he accident prone?
25. Does he exhibit regressive forms of behavior?
26. Is he a perfectionist and succeeds academically?
27. Does he appear to be a day dreamer?
28. Has he had a migrant education program (moved a lot)?
29. Has he attended special classes?
30. Has he repeated grades in school?

31. Does he reject all authority figures--school, home, police?
32. Does he defy structures and school rules?
33. What is the sociological culture of his home?
34. Does he live in a broken home situation?
35. Does he appear to be a parentally neglected child?

These are only a few of the characteristics that may be manifested by a child who is having emotional problems. These characteristics should not be considered in sequence, nor should a child have to possess a certain number of characteristics in order to be disturbed. A determination of his functioning level must be related to the seriousness of his actions, the frequency of his behavior, and whether the behavior lasts over a period of time that appears to be excessive. Most importantly, though, do not take one symptom, and from that behavior determine that the child is disturbed.

All the above authors to whom I have referred were cited from Exceptional Children, Psychological-Survey by Wm. R. Van Osdol and Don Shane, W. C. Brown, Kendall-Hunt Publishing Company, Dubuque, Iowa, 1972.

The Home

In today's society, the family is the major source for a child's socialization. Family life provides the foundation for later development of personality structures, self attitudes, and life styles, (Blackman, 1967).

Since World War II, society has become mobile

because families h a v e n o t been established in one community very long. Families have been fragmented, and f a m i l y ties have been fragile. Parents have f e l t material possessions could protect t h e m from the fears a n d anxieties o f a tension-ridden world. Thus, parent's unsatisfied needs, conflicts, feelings of inadequacy, a n d unfulfilled aspirations h a v e o f t e n b e e n translated i n t o expectations and goals for their child, (Szurek, 1965).

The parent's attitudes toward t h e school and t h e preparation g i v e n t o a child before entering school, can help a child avoid failure, (NEA, 1966). If a child became emotionally unstable before entering school, t h e cause may have been the home environment. I f anything had interfered with a child s satisfactions, and if anything had produced tension; he may have become emotionally disturbed. Emotional disturbance, then may be caused before the child began school. The school, t h o u g h , could become an agent which will increase the tension, (Lippman, 1955).

Although a c h i l d seems to accept being pushed and engineered, h e may dislike being urged a n d exhorted. H e realizes that he must function within a system of being nagged and directed. Constant nagging, pushing for perfection, or holding with detachment, could cause an emotional disturbance. A child will show the results of parental attitudes and anxieties early in his life. He will seek gratification and satisfaction for the things he does. The absence of affectional w a r m t h causes the child t o f e e l unloved. Sheer neglect on the part of the parents, or a lack of sympathetic understanding, makes t h e child feel he is not wanted. Studies h a v e revealed that

31

deprivation in early years, whether cultural or affectional, has affected the development of a child. Failure to develop h a s lead to problems in both learning
and behavior, (Brown, 1968). A child who has been deprived o f h i s parent's love, h a s learned early to
think only of himself. S i n c e he has not been the
primary concern o f his parents; h e feels no one has
been concerned about him. Even though, being deprived
o f a parent's affections h a s affected a child emotionally; in order t o g r o w up and mature, a child
needs to attain a sense of individuality and separate-
ness from his parents, (Ginott, 1969).

When the most vulnerable child has been exposed
t o anxiety o r aggression i n the family, he may be
affected emotionally. An inability to compete successfully gives t h e child a feeling of inferiority.
In a n attempt t o escape from t h e competition, the
child refuses t o cope with difficulties; therefore
escaping, h e i s able to maintain his self-esteem,
(Brown, 1968).

A number o f unfortunate home conditions bring
a b o u t emotional maladjustment in children. Conditions in the home play an important role in developing a child's personality. The home gives the child
the feeling of security t h a t grows from affection.
The home environment provides a basis for achievement.

Family conflicts seem to be greater in the homes
of poor readers than in the homes of children with no
reading difficulties. Therefore, an unfavorable home
condition aggravates school learning problems, b u t
the home situation may not be the only source of the
child's maladjustment. Stressful h o m e situations
cause a child to develop nervous tensions a n d to be-

come a chronic worrier. The home situation causes the child to develop a defeatist attitude. He may quit trying to learn.

There seems to be evidence to support the fact that underachievers generally have lived in privileged homes, or at least in average homes. Very little research has indicated that the majority of underachievers have lived in a so-called bad home. In a majority of incidents, then, while the home has been a "good" home by sociological standards; psychologically it has been an inferior home. Even though the quality of a family's life has been important; the most telling influences on a child may often be quite subtle.

The Parents

Observation and research seem to indicate that a disturbed parent-child relationship is the most frequent primary cause of children's problems. When the emotional bond between parent and child has been disturbed, serious emotional disturbances result. Parents are the most influential source in a child's life, especially before the age of five. A parent's actions and demands effect the whole growth of the child.

At James Jackson Putnam Children's Center in Boston, a research team considered that parents who demanded that a child behave in an idealized adult-like manner were helping to produce the child's difficulties, (Brown, 1968). Child rearing practices of parents have been oriented by certain cultural norms. Parents' child-rearing methods have been influenced by their own personality structures. Parents past lives play an important role in the way they rear their children. If past experiences have left the parents with feelings of inadequacy, or with emotional conflicts; they encounter difficulties in rearing their child. If parents' childhood experiences with their parents were happy, they have a tendency to rear their children accordingly, (Blackham, 1967). Many parents have had feelings of insecurity because they were raised during the depression, and subsequent war years. If they received little attention or concern from their parents, they seem to have little to give their own children.

Some parents unconsciously get their children to act out feelings which they, the parents, cannot do. They provoke children into destructive actions which result from their parents' own fears or impulses. Many times a dual purpose may be served by such actions. The parents' forbidden impulses have been acted out vicariously by the unfortunate child, and through the acting out, the parents' attitude toward the child has been unconsciously changed, (Szurek, 1965).

A child sometimes is partially rejected by his parents. Rarely is a child totally rejected by the parents. Many of the child's emotional conflicts stem from his search for satisfactions which cannot be found at home. Any parent who is overemotional, overprotective, childish, alcoholic, seductive, rejecting, or overconscientious, has difficulty managing sound characteristics for the development of his child, (Ginott, 1969).

The parents' marital relationship affects the child. If the child is caught in a conflict between his parents, his behavior is affected. A parent may detest a trait in the child, because the same trait was prevalent in the parent. Consequently the child may be used as a "pawn" in the parents' battles.

More prevalent in society today are parents who feel material goods are a substitute for relationships. They do not provide their children with the loving care essential for growth. Therefore, some parents feel they have to bribe their child into doing things from fear that he will give up completely. The parents may insist upon exercising detailed guidance in all of the child's activities. When this happens, the child develops a sense of dependency upon the parents to the extent that he is unable to proceed on his own in any learning situation. The overprotective and domineering parents cause the child to have adjustment difficulties. The negative attitudes and suggestions offered by parents consciously or unconsciously invite anti-social behavior. A constant "don't" without follow-up, emphasizes the negative. Thoughtless remarks of failure intensify the fear of failure in a child, (NEA, 1966).

Parents reactions to aggressive behavior affect the child's attitudes. The inability of parents to set limits on aggressive behavior often reflects their own anxieties about such behavior. They receive satisfaction from their actions toward the child because the child does something the parent would like to do, but would dare not, (Szurek, 1965).

Parents often force a child to study, and hopefully he will achieve. A revision needs to be made in the way the parents pressure the child. If homework and high grades became diamonds in his parents' crown, the child may prefer to bring home a crown of work that would at least be his own. By his not having attained his parents' goals, the child rebel achieves a sense of independence. Thus, Ginott (1969) felt that the need for individuality and uniqueness could push a child into failure, regardless of parental pressure and punishment.

Parents can help their child in school by cooperating with his teacher. Parents usually know their child as an individual, but the teacher has a special knowledge of normal behavior of children in his age group. If the parent condemns the teacher and her methods in the presence of the child; the child, in all probability, will make no further effort in his school work. By not performing, he will be fulfilling his desire to prove that his teacher was wrong, and his parents were right. The child will benefit only when the parent and teacher work together. If a parent encourages his child's efforts, applaud his successes, and ignores his failures; learning should become a source of pleasure for the child.

In many ways, a parent helps his child develop a healthy mental attitude. Parents need to like their child, but they should not have an urgent need to be liked by him every minute of the day. When parents understand how important their help is to the child; they will feel better about themselves as effective parents. The child will then begin to change when the parents listen with sensitivity, and suspend the cutting comments. Therefore, when parents' feelings and requirements are given without insult, change will occur, (Ginott, 1969).

A parent needs to be realistic in setting goals for his child. When a child is doing his best, he has a right to feel successful, but if the goals are set too high, he will fail. A child can never be successful all the time, and parents have to convey the fact to the child that everyone fails sometimes.

Mother and fathers will continue to have trouble with their children, because the best parents don't seem to be quite good enough. No certain amount of knowledge or wisdom on the part of the parents will guarantee that their children will develop normally. Parents have their share of frailty, but they must meet the challenge of a child who is not like themselves. The world in which their children grow is not like the one in which the parents grew. Children do not live in a small environment surrounded by only mother and father. Parents must be brave enough to hold the child to reasonable standards of performance. They must also accept the child as himself. If parents are willing to accept the child as he is; the child will gravitate toward the values of the parents and grow to be a well developed child. It is important for parents to realize that there is no one cause for emotional problems. Causes for emotional maladjustment may be physical, economic, social, mental, or any combination of these.

When the basic drives and natural desires of children are thwarted, and these drives and desires are not directed into other constructive areas, the child is likely to build up tensions and distress which may cause emotional problems. Some environmental conditions in the home which may cause emotional problems are as follows:

1. Too much pressure from parents to succeed.
2. Comparisons with other members of the family who are more successful in school and activities.
3. Parents who are really adult children and quarrel with each other and are unable to maintain adequate discipline.
4. Many pupils feel that they are not loved and that they do not belong.
5. Congested living conditions, which prevent individuals from being alone.
6. Overprotective parents who will not let their children grow up, by showering them with too much attention and too many material things, and do not require the children to assume responsibility.
7. Broken homes which may exist even if both parents are living at home.

Today the approach to helping the emotionally disturbed child has changed from trying to determine the etiology, to attempting to find an effective way to control or modify the situation. Structured activities help to bring a child out of isolation and into contact with others. These activities can provide the child with growing confidence and success if carefully selected. An atmosphere which attempts to build up confidence should be maintained. In order to have a feeling of belonging, children should be allowed to participate in family decisions, share their feelings of joy and sorrow, and feel confident in giving and receiving love. This is of the utmost importance in attaining good emotional adjustment.

It is very important for the child to realize that it is normal not to be perfect. All people make mistakes for which they are sorry, but they should not continually feel ashamed and punished themselves. Parents of the emotionally disturbed child need to make the child feel that he is accepted as an individual, and that his behavior will be met with understanding.

He needs an environment which will permit him to express his emotions, whatever they may be, without censure; to control these emotions realistically within the framework of what is considered socially acceptable; and to provide himself with opportunities for possible insight into his own behavior. The disturbed child who is aggressive is permitted to express his aggression without harming himself or others; while the withdrawn child is not pressured into socializing, but is treated with intelligent neglect.

The emotionally disturbed child has much hostility and will attempt at every opportunity to test the limits of his parents and other authority figures. It is necessary to try to relieve the child's concept that authority is a threatening force. Little by little the child will begin to realize that perhaps nothing he can do will break the family relationship, while at the same time he becomes aware that his behavior is considered socially unacceptable. It is necessary for the child to feel that no matter what he does he is accepted and liked as an individual even though there is disapproval of his behavior at particular times.

Emotionally d i s t u r b e d children n e e d order,
structure, and defined limits in their daily lives.
They welcome a n d respect firmness, and like to know
what their limits are.   Freedom a n d choice c a n be
e x e r c i s e d within the limits.   This provides the
child w i t h the security he needs. Any approach to
working w i t h the emotionally disturbed child needs
con tinuity a n d consistency.   These approaches need
to be developed a n d maintained b y both parents and
teachers.

The School

The most withdrawn and alienated child will begin to
respond through educational measures. When he begins
t o achieve academically, h i s fears about t h e outer world will begin to reduce. Teachers are a m a z ed
with the progress of an emotionally disturbed c h i l d
when he begins to learn.

    T e a c h e r s are overwhelmed at the restlessness,
temper outbursts, short attemtion span, hostility,
and indifference of a child.   If a child feels someone owes him something; he d o e s not understand why
he should do the work necessary for learning. It is
easier for him t o drift, a n d to let others do t h e
worrying, rather t h a n put forth the effort himself.
Veteran t e a c h e r s say they have never encountered
so many youngsters w h o have had so little desire or
interest to learn, (Szurek, 1965).

    H e l p can be given to an emotionally disturb e d
child.   To help, though, smaller classes will have
to exist.   The teacher needs to recognize how important learning is to the c h i l d.   T h e relationship
with the teacher is a vital part of a child's learn-

ing. The teacher has to be concerned for the child. A child will try hard for one who believes that his best is good enough. When a teacher persists through all the child's trying, protests, hostilities, and indifferences; t h e student will begin t o believe that someone cares. If the child has not experienced achievement very many times; the expression of pleasure from the teacher toward t h e child's achievement will be v e r y important to the child. The evidence shown by the teacher's p l e a s u r e in the student's learning is vital to the continuation and success of the work of the child.

Through guidance a child may turn his e x p e r i- ences of failure into constructive i d e a s.   O n l y through learning can a child begin to feel more secure about himself. The therapeutic role of education for the child is very important. Successful school work will not solve all his problems, but he will begin to f e e l that he i s a more competent, effective, and hopeful individual.

Therapy is the specialist's business, m e n t a l hygiene is everyone's business.   A teacher's class- room practices can do much toward helping her pupils emotionally to be well.   T h e following suggestions are some principles which you c a n use a s a guide: Make sure your c l a s s r o o m is a bright cheerf ul, friendly place. Children, t h e same a s adults, are susceptable to t h e i r physical surroundings.   Y o u probably cannot repaint your room, but you can cover the walls with richly colored reproductions of famous pictures and have a changing panorama o f children's drawings. Keep the vases in the room full of flowers. Cover the library table with books and magazines t o display illustrations. A well-arranged room invites children to new experiences, exhibits of apparatus, and collections; really accessible art materials and bulletin boards with clippings of current events stir children's interest and make them eager to learn, (Cutts, 1961).

A teacher's own temperament sets the emotional tone of a room. The teacher should be cheerful and friendly and show a personal interest in each child. The child should regard the teacher as a friend to whom he can express his feelings. Teachers should pay attention to their own personal appearances.

The teacher of the emotionally disturbed child should be a person who is emotionally mature, well grounded in education and psychology, talented in arts, has a wide range of interests, and with all these attributes is aware of personal limitations. Teachers who are the most successful with emotionally disturbed children are genuine human beings who have insights into their own needs and have the capacity to become part of a treatment team, (Berkowitz, 1960).

Making positive statements about factors of teacher personality as they relate to successful teaching of emotionally disturbed children is a risky business. Conflicts exist in the total area of thought and also in the philosophical differences of how to teach these children. At the same time, there are certain definable traits that tend to show relatively good immediate results in special class teaching.

1. A calmness in the way they respond to and deal with the problems and conflicts of children.

2. An unshakable stability in all phases of the child-teacher relationship.
3. An attitude of fairness and sincerity with children.
4. A firm belief in the potential of all children.
5. An unyielding firmness in holding limits once set and clearly defined.
6. The ability to apply and direct teaching materials in an orderly manner. (Haring, 1962).

An examination of several recent investigations supports classroom procedures based upon structure involving consistent realistic expectations. The teacher who, in addition to working in the structured classroom environment, carefully plans and organizes the presentation of materials with an attitude of high work orientation, fares better in terms of the behavior and academic progress of normal children.

Educational considerations of importance in controlling the hyperactivity and distractibility of children might be summed up in the following suggestions:

1. Reduce all extraneous stimuli.
2. Reduce excessive physical activity during study periods.
3. Detail methods and add order to materials to be learned.
4. Increase the stimulus value of materials to be learned.
5. Follow step by step sequences in presently complex materials.
6. Insist upon accuracy of work.

43

7. Prevent unnecessary or careless failure to do work acceptably, (Haring, 1962).

Relations between the therapist and the school are an essential aspect of psychotherapy for the children. Through school visits, the therapist can understand the nature of an experience which represents a major part of the child's life. Contact with the school makes it possible for the therapist to present to the teacher basic themes, dynamics, and understanding attitudes in the child's behavior. The therapist's attitude in visiting the school need not be that of a consultant or advisor. His basic interest can be to understand the school philosophy and practice, and how it affects the child as well as to give information which may eventuate a positive school experience for the child. The therapist's relationship with the teacher is also an opportunity, not only to foster a healthy approach to the child in the classroom, but also to gain an understanding of the realities with which the classroom teacher must live, (Moustakas, 1959).

The following list is devoted to suggestions, (Do's or Dont's) related to the emotional needs of children in the classroom.

1. Don't be casual about absences of children who have unmet emotional needs.
2. Don't think of him as a completely integrated person who does not heed those little words of reassurance.
3. Don't try to avoid the children.
4. Don't brush off their efforts to make contact with you.
5. Don't neglect their ideas.

6. Don't be too obvious in pushing some of these children away from you so you can talk more readily with another child.

7. Don't t r y to make the school room situation a place in which everything is cut and dried. Children l e a r n through trying things a n d making mistakes, just as we do.

8. Because they are small or young, don't m a k e the mistake of thinking that they don't need the feeling of importance. They love to feel that they are a part o f things that are going on.

9. Don't point h i m out as, "The only o n e who hasn't followed the rules, o r w ho h a s spoiled the record of absences or tardiness, or who is the only noisy one."

10. Don't ridicule them or embarrass them.

11. Don't mistrust him before a group.

12. Don't e v e r tell other children o r other teachers something that a child has told you in confidence.

13. Don't ever overlook his need for belonging.

14. Don't have children work "just for you." T r y to have them develop some purpose. Don't let rewards and punishments reflect your personal acceptance or rejection. You want their rewards to come out of their experiences, rather than from you as a person.

15. Don't t r y to h a v e children do t h i n g s or avoid things just because of fear. Help them to see that the use of their intelligence in a situation is their best aid.

16. Don't try to handle deep psychological prob-

lems of children. Don't try to function as a psychiatrist or analyst.

17. Don't keep the pressure on children a l l day long. Don't have them concentrating at all times on intensive work. Do have a variety in the daily life of the child. Don't always be suggesting goals, penalties, or rewards. Don't communicate the ideas, "Hurry, hurry, or you won't get done."

18. Don't withdraw from children who want to be loving and kind. T r y to be as accepting as you can.

19. Avoid giving children the impression t h a t their particular problems are of no concern to you. When children lie, steal, or cheat; don't make a great public ado about it. Don't humiliate or debase them, (Raths, 1963).

Your efforts should always be consciously directed toward promoting a feeling of belonging. The activities you choose t o accomplish i t must somehow or other, be enveloped in an atmosphere of warmth and friendliness. After you have that point of view you will see many additional things to do and to avoid in order to promote inner emotional security.

The teacher

So you're a teacher of a class of emotionally troubled children, who, for the most part, have learning and behavioral problems. There are many personality factors influencing learning and beha v i o r a l patterns which are indispensably important ingredients in the way a child uses his intellectual potential.

In taking a moment to look at some of these characteristics, I would like to begin with curiosity. Curiosity is an intrinsic part of the child's personality--to see how things work out, or are put together, or taken apart, as the case may be. Many factors influence this desire, but certain experiences in life may curtail its fullfillment. A child, under threat of parental rejection, for instance, may have had exploratory behavior subdued through insistence of overconformity. Such fears may generalize into all areas of his behavior.

A child is persistent--that is, he is free to use his energies to pursue school tasks, to attack problems, and to challenge unclear material. This aggressiveness is sometimes inhibited because it is unrealistically associated with danger--danger of failure, danger of injury.

Positive identification means the desire to imitate important adult behavior, plus the need to please and be respected by important people in the child's life. It is the ability of the child to feel positive toward his teacher and the desire to imitate him. Identification, too, is dependent upon preschool experiences.

The child needs, for maximum development of his potential, independence of thought. Its counterpart, complete acceptance of taught material, results in parroted learning. The problem usually increases as the child moves through school. The ability to tolerate a disagreeable task to achieve a goal can be a painful process, but it is necessary if the child is to stick with a learning problem and use his abilities to solve that problem.

The ability to concentrate is self-explanatory. Chronic or transient disabilities may result from lack of concentration; therefore, three factors are implicated. Unmet basic needs may not allow a child to seek solutions to academic problems. Unresolved inner conflicts, preoccupation with sexual identity, or sibling rivalry often precludes problems of concentration.

Anything that enriches these characteristics, increases the effective use of the child's promising intelligence. Conversely, anything that intrudes into the growth of these characteristics, retards the intellectual potential.

Where do you as a teacher fit into this picture? In view of professionalism, a teacher is first a teacher. This is not to deny the therapeutic role in relation to the children with whom she works. A teacher preserves for the child a realistic concept of what school and teacher mean. There is no reason why a teacher cannot be warm and loving; and, she may become a substitute mother to some children. She can have fun and laugh with the children, but she must know the limits if she expects her students to know theirs. The teacher cannot, while being companionable, forget that she is not a member of the peer group. These suggestions are normal expectations for any teacher, but they are even more significant in dealing with the emotionally disturbed.

The classroom should be as nearly like a regular classroom as possible. This allows the children to test the physical limits of the room to see if it offers security. This allows them to recognize it as a classroom--they are doing school work just as they had d o n e in regular schoolrooms. This allows them t o interact w i t h other children through group work, helping y o u n g e r children, and doing class-room tasks that benefit all.

You are a teacher, y o u have t h e children, you have the room. I n what direction do you go? Cer-tainly goals are necessary. I h a v e found certain goals are significant i n giving direction to teach-ing: (1) To show the child th at he can find accep-tance by adults and peers through acceptable behavior, and at t h e s a m e time recognize that unacce ptable behavior is calling attention to some need. (2) To show the child that he can be accepted by others with-outbeing aggressive, solicitous, infantile, or pr o -fane. (3) T o help h i m develop appropriate ways of handling his f e e l i n g s. (4) To help him live through periods of anxiety. (5) To help the child accept school as not a place to f e a r --that he will be accepted at his level of maturity and achievement --and that he can have his share of academic success.

Progress i s v e r y slow, the regressions a r e certainly frustrating, but is's great to see a child moving in a positive direction. The mutual communi-cation, the support and planning among all staff per-sonnel involved are required and indispensible compo-nents in the positive movements of your students.

Children a s k--more o f t e n demand--that limits be set f o r t h e m. Often these demands come in the form o f inappropriate behavior, and then discipline rears its u g l y head. Warning f l a g s usually are flown; b u t if the teacher is aware of the approach-ing storm, i t c a n sometimes b e quieted. I f the assignment is causing the anxiety; change the assignment to one around which the child is more comfortable. If the distractive behavior of another child is causing the anxiety; let the youngster leave the room--get a drink of water; take a short walk, or run an errand. With discretion, the teacher may choose to use humor as his means of reducing frustrating or anxious moments. Humor is very effective with some children and certainly makes the classroom atmosphere more delightful and eliminates the additional stress that often accompanies visual or verbal warnings. If the anxiety is such that it will not allow the child to respond to tension-reducing methods, other action must be pursued. Very often isolation from the group is effective-- isolation from the existing stimuli, but isolation should be near an adult, such as a teacher's aid, who will be accessible to the child.

In any event, and most importantly is the principle that the discipline methods should be tailored to fit the individual and the situation. A knowing look at Sue may be sufficient, but George may need a firm hand on his shoulder and a few words to let him know he is misbehaving. Disciplinary methods--or better yet--behavioral management methods--should allow that which each of us needs at times--that is, to "save face." Only when the child is in danger of harming the teacher, others in the class, or himself does he need the protection of physical restraint. Discipline must be of a uniform and realistic nature. It must allow the child to express his anxiety or hostility within reasonable bounds providing it is helpful to the child and does not take on the aspect of rejection on the part of the teacher.

Punishment may be administered either physically

or psychologically by the teacher through presentation of painful stimuli or through withdrawal of pleasant stimuli. Punishment, generally though does not eliminate the poor behavior, but it does usually slow down the rate of emission of behavior. Also, it should be noted that punishment probably does not show the child appropriate behavior, but it does give notice that the child should stop poor behavior. Therefore, punishment may be limitingly effective.

Additional suggestions for teachers and co-workers would be to reinstate the original trauma through a soft approach for re-learning. An example may be for the child who is severely traumatized by 40 arithmetic problems. The teacher could start the child by helping him successfully complete one problem, then two, then three; and hopefully reinstate a learning situation through success, rather than creating trauma through failure.

The teacher, also may help the child to solve his interpersonal problems by interaction with the teacher and other children. This problem cannot be solved, though, if the teacher yells and screams at the child for his personal inabilities. The child with problems needs a confidence builder, not a person who humiliates. Certain teacher feedback to the child through good behavior modeling, and the teaching of behavior control by using appropriate words for different roles, enables the child to learn and to use tools which contribute to his social and academic growth.

teachers should help children to create new habits that will interfere with the old, undesirable habits, the possible repetition of undesirable behavior with neither positive nor negative reinforcement, may enable t h e child to turn-on or turn-off certain behavior. If one learns to turn-on poor behavior at will; he should likewise be able to control his unde- sirable behavior.

The Child

As adults we must realize a child's perspective and not demand that the child adhere t o o u r adult world.   I believe a number of very general concepts about children i n trouble c a n be of great value to the adult who i s having difficulty trying to figure out why a child is a disturbed and troubled child.

We must realize that children who sometimes are in trouble are in trouble because they repeat actions that g e t them into trouble. Many times the actions of the child would not warrant a troubled c o n c ep t if he were in a different home, school, or community environment. Children are troubled because of adult r e a c t i o n s which are constant and hostile to such things as follows: wearing unusual clothes, talking very strangely (n o t obscene), being dirty, acting strangely (but not physically harming people or prop- rty).   I'm not saying we should complacently over- look dirty p h y s i c a l hygiene, etc.; but we do, as adults, sometimes overreact t o t h e young person's world.

Youngsters do get into serious trouble sometimes when t h e y are doing poorly in school, quit school, quit working, using drugs or alcohol, trying to com- mit suicide, physically abusing themselves (burns with cigaretts, cutting initials on arms, etc.), breaking laws, sexually misbehaving, running away from home , or by simply being unhappy and withdrawn into a fantasy world.

If we hope to help these kids, we must be aware of the many things that constitute the image of a child's troubled world. These children usually are very unhappy. They believe that adults are inconsistent and hypocritical. (Are we?) They are told different things by different adults and they cannot discern who is right. They do not understand the work that their parents do, and also realize that their parents don't even respect their own jobs and work. Many troubled children have never seen a happy adult. (Where are you, Mr. and Mrs. Adult?) Children in trouble seldom get to see or talk with an adult alone. (Have you given your child that opportunity lately?) Some children do not even know many adults. (Should children be seen and not heard?) These kids are sometimes even punished by their own peers for staying out of trouble, and they get no rewards from adults for good behavior. They do get serious attention, though, from adults when they get into trouble. Children with problems think they can't change, and strangely enough, we adults agree with them. Troubled children see little reason why they should be any other way. They are bored and don't believe they can do anything, or know how to do anything. They don't like themselves or very many other people. They believe they are totally bad, but they have very ordinary ideas about what is right and wrong.

Now, take a good look at this troubled and dis-

turbed child. How do you really see this child?
"Shape up. Do right. Get your grades. Get a j o b,
or out you go." Picture the child with problems and
then try to understand that he has many unmet needs,
and you as parents and teachers can help this troubled
child. He needs to feel that he is worth something.
He needs adults who will force or let him make decisions for himself, and can help him overcome the bad
decisions that he does make. He needs to know that
y o u are not so weak that y o u need him to need you.
He needs to know that y o u understand that haircuts,
clothing, a n d teenage rituals are somewhat trivial;
and that you will let him know that knowledge, self-
control, and ability are important, but not paramount.
He needs t o know that y o u can tell him "no" fairly,
consistently, and mean it. He needs to know that y ou
will attend to those things he does well, and are not
interested o n l y in his failures. He needs to know
that you respect him, e v e n though you a r e unhappy
with h i s inappropriate behavior. He needs to know
t h a t you are genuinely interested in children. He
needs to know adults who will speak to him courteous-
ly. He needs t o know that you will listen to him.
He needs to develop skills and use them. He needs to
feel that a change i n his life is worth making, and
he needs t o know that he can change himself and the
circumstances around him.

Again, parents and teachers, d o you enable the
young people around you to meet and enjoy t h e needs
that are so essential to good mental health? If not
take a good survey of y o u r awareness and practices
a n d t r y to turn around the misery that may exist
within some child.

Relationships in Therapeutic Settings

Some aspects of relationships between t e a c her and child, psychotherapist and child, and teacher and psychotherapist may differ qualitatively; while other aspects, though similar in nature, may differ quantitatively. Parents and teachers need to recognize the therapeutic relationship between teacher a n d child which can lead to social and emotional growth as well as academic progress; and be careful to make the distinction between educationally therapeutic and psychotherapeutic roles. Although I will place emphasis on teacher and child, for a frame of reference, I wish to set up operational definitions of t h e s e three types of relationships.

Certain elements may be thought to characterize psychotherapy. Paramount is the prolonged interpersonal relationship between t w o or more people with attention focused o n an individual who is suffering emotional and/or s o c i a l distress. Those elements seem to imply interaction with and involvement of the patient. The psychological method implemented b y a procedure based on formal theory is carried out by a person, labeled psychotherapist, who has specialized experiences or t r a i n i n g in human relations. It should be his and his patient's m u t u a l aim that, through this process involving the evaluation of the s e l f , amelioration of t h e difficulties w i ll b e attained.

One of the first requirements for a therapeutic relationship between teacher and child is the teacher's faith in h e r ability to be therapeutic. This faith may or may not be at her level of awareness. Frequently the teacher does not see her methods in this light, but s e e s therapy as something extraneous to t h e learning situation. I t is important that she know that she can set up a relationship with a child either spontaneously or systematically. Meeting the needs of children in the classroom is a kind of educational therapy, and the more flexible and creative the teacher is in discerning and meeting real needs; t h e more likely she will be able to ameliorate present learning problems and to forestall new ones.

The steps taken succeeding t h e perception o f social or emotional problems b y psychotherapist and teacher differ largely in whether the emphasis is on the historical or situational conflict respectively. T h e teacher, in dealing with the situation at hand, offers her support and realistic help around inappropriate behavior patterns without becoming involved with internalized difficulties. She may affect this by strengthening healthy defenses a n d b y offering tolerable and reality-based substitutes f o r t hose pressures which bring about disturbed behavior. This procedure is in contrast to t h e psychotherapist who may attempt to give insight into the nature of defenses, and to free t h e child of internal needs for the disturbed behavior. Perhaps the most important difference is that the relationship between teacher and c h i l d exists with management of p r e s e nt problems instead of interpretation of past experiences; whereas, that which is between psychotherapist and child usually takes both into consideration.

Finally, the need f o r reciprocal communication between the teacher and psychotherapist c a n n o t be stressed enough. T h e channels for reciprocity may vary according to the working situations--indirectly or directly through the school psychologist i n t h e public school o r through an educational director in a special school setting. The importance of communication grows out of the positive value of integrating the t o t a l treatment process, w i t h the school playing its appropriate role.

Provision is made for the total growth and functioning of the child through t h e comprehensive approach of our schools. A positive school experience c a n be vital in the prevention of maladjustment, a teacher's role must be extended to i nclude the meeting of emotional as well as academic needs of the individual. Needs for success, and acceptable self-concept self-realization, and adequate means for coping with one's problems should be considered. Learning may be facilitated if curiosity, a willingness to t a k e a chance, is fostered. For a child, failure in school may only thwart fulfillment of such needs, which, in turn, impedes growth.

However, before a teacher can successfully meet these emotionally-toned needs, she must have a positive concept o f herself. T his i s especially true when she is considered part of a total therapeutic experience. An empathetic relationship, coupled with appropriate dependency, presupposes t h a t a teacher has the freedom to provide, withhold, and structure, in the give and take milieu between her and the child . O n l y insight into her own needs--her strengths and weaknesses--c a n allow this freedom. Insecurity in the t e a c h e r encourages insecurity in t h e child. Feelings o f inadequacy m a y cause her to see misbehavior as a personal a f f r o n t. At this point, if she allows the child to fail academically, socially or emotionally; his failure becomes a further threat, causing the teacher to exert undue pressure and unconscious hostility upon herself and the children. One should keep in mind that the disturbed child is usually not equipped to manage his own problems, and that a teacher may feel inadequate, when in fact, she has something to offer. As all therapy may not be therapeutic; conversely, a relationship, not denoted as therapy, may be therapeutic. To see oneself as a therapeutic educator, a specialist in one's field, and a member of a team is essential for a positive self-concept. Feeling for this can be encouraged by supervisors in education, psychology, or psychiatry and affirmed by staff relations and attitudes.

Inside the classroom the establishment of a relationship between the teacher and any child becomes an essential tool in opening the way for learning to take place. This is probably even more true when the child is emotionally disturbed. Children who have been rejected emotionally, or who are social or emotional isolates, phobic, withdrawn, acting out, or whose academic success is achieved by their compulsivity and/or constriction need to establish with their teacher a relationship characterized by mutual trust, understanding, and respect. If a child feels that the teacher is a caring individual with special interest in him he will be able to attend school and be receptive to learning. He can begin to work in order to earn love, praise, and approval. Although this motive should not be the ultimate goal; it is the first step in helping a child internalize satisfactions to be gleaned from the work itself. Identification is a key to building this relationship, because it allows teacher and child to sense and gain from the needs of each other. After a positive, healthy, working relationship has been established; motivation may gradually be internalized, and the children may move from work for love to love for work. This relationship may be improved if the children do not receive appraisal of their work by grades, but instead discuss their work with their teacher on a one-to-one basis. In this way a child learns to compete with himself rather than with his peers, and improvement signifies success.

Gains from a positive student-teacher relationship which append academic achievement are those pertaining to ego development. A school, or even a classroom in a clinic, ought to represent reality to the child and to provide room for reality-testing. This can take place in the form of provision of organizing experiences, allowance of feelings which need not be accompanied by guilt, and guidance in impulse-control in appropriate behavior. If mastered by the child, these things may serve as agents to increase his acceptability by peers and adults, who reflect for him an image he uses in the formation of a self-concept.

The establishment of a relationship is not enough. It must be sustained. Daily the teacher reinforces trust as she provides the child with a curriculum that enhances his sense of conpetence for interaction with his environment. Content, as well as method has particular significance for the emotionally disturbed child, and because this is true; interests, needs, abilities, and focus on reality should be considered. This requires the teacher to have knowledge of the strengths and limitations of a child, and thereby to develop her procedures. Hopefully, integration of the learning experience into the personality will result, and the child will be able to give up debilitating defense mechanisms.

In some cases, the credit indicated by content or techniques should be shared with or given totally to a relationship. It may be that the recognition granted remedial instruction belongs to the relationship itself, which represents the willingness of the teacher to help the child. Environmental manipulation, other than content adaptation, may be necessary. This is especially true when the emotional drive needed for motivation is inactive or absent. Stimulation should come from an environment which is free from threat and undue pressure and which insures the availability of pleasure. The child needs to feel that help is available when he needs it, so that he does not have to expend energy unnecessarily in testing people. Rarely should anxiety be induced; more often it should be allayed, even if it means modification of the environment. Flexibility in the daily program must account for the individual's ability level, limitations interest span, and ability to interact with others. Such environmental manipulation implements the work of education and efforts for ego-building. In a special class setting, particular attention is paid to the arrangement of facilities to suit each child based on an understanding of his conflicts and behavior. Although such adjustment is not always feasible in a public school classroom, it may be possible to some degree without much disruption of the regular program and must be thought of as an essential ingredient in a total growth approach to the child.

For those teachers instructing a boy or girl who is receiving psychotherapy privately, in a clinic, or elsewhere; the integration of the educational program into the treatment process is beneficial. It is at this point that reciprocal communication between the teacher, psychotherapist, caseworker, and other individuals in contact with the child is essential so that united and overall goals may be maintained. However necessary this cooperation may be, it is not always a fact. Members of the disciplines of psychiatry, psychology, and social work sometimes look upon educators as interlopers in the area of treatment, or are at least uncomfortable with using information or personnel from the school to any great extent in their management of a case. On the other hand, the educator may see himself as an interloper or a layman with little to offer the psychotherapeutic team. This may be the point at which treatment breaks down. Information concerning the child's feelings about the classroom--learning, his peers, and adults--imparted by the teacher can provide the psychotherapist with a rich supply of material which could expedite the treatment process and make it a more meaningful experience for the child.

Acknowledging the reality of this situation, members of the interested professions are attempting to come to grips with the problem of how to effect this interdisciplinary association. Naturally, the degree practicable varies depending upon whether one's work is done in a clinic, residential, or public school setting. Professionals need to recognize the total program as therapeutic, and affectively fostered mutual respect between disciplines and keep open constant lines of communication. All persons should recognize the specialized ability of each member of the treatment team and the vital comtribution that he or she can make to the total functioning of the child. In consonance with this attitude, they should encourage participation of the total staff in scheduled meetings for disposition and re-evaluation of cases and in the planning for a particular child. Each staff member should be recognized as a professional responsible for satisfactory execution of his task as well as for making a didactic contribution concerning his own field which will benefit his fellow workers.

Such feelings promoted in adults concerned with treatment, benefit the child. Attitudes derived from fellow workers and from one's own sense of worth and competence stimulate a desire to help the child. In addition, the youth may realize for the first time that his parents care enough for him to try to do something about his problem and he may perceive that a whole team of people are working together for his welfare. The teacher who imparts information to the child's psychotherapist and to the parents' caseworker about the student's classroom activities, also communicates to the student that what he is doing is important to someone; likewise, informing the parents of a child's behavior may provide an opportunity to manifest their feelings of caring for the child, which can bring a family closer together. Ultimately, the child may be able to do this communicating directly. Until this is possible, only a treatment team with a positive working relationship can assure the necessary communication of pertinent information to those concerned with the care of the patient.

Relationships, then, are a key to effective treatment of emotionally disturbed children and communication is an essential tool in establishing these relationships. Educators and the psychotherapeutic team must feel the need for this relationship and work to insure its existence. Each individual must be constantly aware of the effectiveness of the relationships between teacher and child, psychothera- pist and child, and teacher and psychotherapist, and personally strive to see that cooperation becomes a reality.

Out-Patient Treatment

Out-patient treatment is found in such settings as mental health clinics and out-patient departments of mental institutions. The patient is generally seen for one or two hours and returns home. This setting offers somewhat more of a total program than the private practitioners, such as psychological personnel, social workers, speech therapists, and others. The child can keep in contact with his family while in an out-patient facility, although this procedure could be a disadvantage as well. The cost in such a setting is generally not as expensive as private therapy, because many of these centers receive some community aid or may be totally supported.

Residential Treatment

Let us look for a moment at the residential treatment centers for disturbed children. The advantage here, as in the out-patient service, is that a total program of services is generally available. Again, the cost is generally born predominantly by the state or some other governmental agency. One of the disadvantages of the residential institution is that there is loss of contact with home and community. This loss of home contact may also be an advantage as well, if his family is a major contributor to his disturbance.

Day Hospital Program

The day hospital is a facility to which children come to spend the full day to receive not only concentrated psychological therapy, but also, educational and medical service. The child is able to keep contact with his environment, and can go home in the evening to test his progress or failure. The day hospital offers an opportunity for intensive counseling and therapy with parents. It is obvious that it has an advantage over some of the programs mentioned above, because it does provide total treatment and educational services. Unlike residential institutions, it does not need the funds for twenty-four hour care.

This brief discussion of psychiatric settings was not to point to the superiority of one over the other. The setting will depend upon the degree of disturbance, the facilities available in the area, the financial status of the parents or agency, and many other factors

Overview

The first section of this b o o k has introduced s o m e w h a t the conditions associated with emotional disturbances.   T h e information is n o t intended to be comprehensive in theory or practice.   Hopefully, though, the reader will have received an introduction to the world of the emotionally disturbed child, but simultaneously t h e   r e a d e r should not believe that a l l questions h a v e been answered.   There is a vast amount of theory, procedures, and clinical approaches directed toward the program f o r disturbed children. You have only received a survey o r   a n   acquaintance with disturbed children; therefore, p l e a s e no not f e e l that y o u are competent to remediate all disturbed problems.

Section two of this book will be concerned with s o m e specific suggestions f o r certain   behavioral situations. These suggestions should b e   helpful   t o those w h o   work with "normal" children   and/or with disturbed children.

BIBLIOGRAPHY

Berkowitz, Pearl H. and Roth an, Ester P.,   The Disturbed Child Recognition a n d Psychoeducational Therapy in the Classroom,   New York,   New York University Press, 1960.

Blackham, Garth J.   T h e Deviant Child in the Classroom.   Belmont, California: Wadsworth Publishing Company, Inc., 1967.

Brown, Bertuam S., "Early Signs of Antisocial Behavior," PTA Magazine, LXII (March, 1968),

Cutts, Norma E., Providing for Individual Differences. New Jersey, Prentice-Hall, 1961.

Ginott, Hiam G., Between Parent and Child. New York: The MacMillan Company, 1969.

Haring, Norris G., and Phipps E. Lakin, Educating Emotionally Disturbed Children. New York, McGraw-Hill Book Co., Inc., 1962.

Lippman, Hyman S., A Treatment of the Child in Emotional Conflict. New York: McGraw-Hill Book Co., Inc., 1956.

Moustakas, E. Clark, Psychotherapy With Children. New York: Harper & Brothers, 1959.

"Parents Can Help: Excerpts from Prevention of Failure," NEA Journal, LV (April, 1966),

Raths, Louis Edward, Understanding The Problem Child. Oklahoma City, Okla., Economy Company, 1963.

Szurek, S. A., Learning and Its Disorders in Berlin. Palo Alto, California: Science and Behavior Books, Inc., 1965.

Van Osdol, Wm. R., and Shane, Don G., Exceptional Children, Psychology-Survey. Kendall/Hunt, W.C. Brown Company, 1972.

SECTION TWO

PSYCHOLOGICAL BEHAVIOR

The subject o f this conversation i s concerned
with t h e manifestation o f maternal deprivation --
infantile autism. In infantile a u t i s m t h e child
seems t o have no affective awareness of other human
beings. Behavior which suggests perception and awareness that mother is absent. There appears to b e a
total lack of contact with the outside world. An example of this is a statement by a mother of an autistic child, "She never made any personal contact or
appeal for help at any time."

Infantile autism is probably a childhood psychosis in which the child lacks any capacity to trust or
communicate with other individuals. The child may
also be either mute or may have complex disturbances
of speech, and could easily be diagnosed as mentally
defective if it were not f o r h i s ability to handle
inanimate objects. Some psychiatrists believe autism
seems to be the basic defense attitude of 'the infant.
It seems as though they cannot tolerate stimulation
from the outer would as well as they master their inner isolated feelings. T h e i r thought process e s,
their highly selective and restricted sensory awareness seem to overtax their concept of self.

Bernard Rimland (1964) has a quite th o ro u g h
formulation of the symptoms of an autistic child. He
feels very strongly that the child neither looks, nor
is mentally retarded. However, h e says that t h e
child may appear retarded socially, because of h i s

inability to form relationships. The first inclination by the parent that the child is autistic may be the lack of the usual anticipatory movements by the child prior to being held. Also, there is often stiffness or failure to make the usual adjustments of his body to adapt to the person carrying or holding him. There are other disturbing symptoms which appear around the fourth to eighteenth months such as prolonged rocking, head banging, apathy and disinterest, unusual fear of strangers, obsessive interest in certain toy or mechanical appliances, highly repetitive and ritualistic play, insistence on being left alone, not changing the physical environment, very unusual language behavior, self-imposed isolation or "autistic aloneness," odd eating habits, and suspected deafness. Of the above listed symptoms, Rimland believes that self-imposed isolation and insistance on the preservation of sameness are two of the most widely accepted diagnostic signs.

The speech of the autistic child, if he speaks at all, is very distinctive and indicative of pathology. The autistic child does not learn to speak in monosyllables like "mama" and "dada" and "car;" but will remain mute until his emotional state has reached a point at which he is ready to resume speech. He will then begin by repeating a whole phrase or sentence, the organization of which is commensurate with the general intellectual level at which he is functioning.

The failute to hear, or more explicitely, the failure to respond to auditory stimuli is part of the child's withdrawal. It is evident that in a large proportion of autistic children, the apparent deafness is probably because of auditory avoidance. They also tend to show visual avoidance by just closing their eyes. Autistic children frequently fail to respond to tactile stimuli. When they are in a severly withdrawn state, freqently another person m a y touch a child in order to attract his attention, but no response from the child is evoked. These children have not lost the sense of touch or the ability to feel things; because at times it is quite obvious t h a t they can f e e l things normally and they make great u s e of their tactile senses i n manipulat ing familiar objects. Many children derive pleasure from the feel of surfaces and textures.

It is suggested that these children, having little interest in the world and its people, turn toward their own bodies an d their primitive sensory satisfactions. Ultimately, of course, the deviant behavior in childhood autism must b e the result of some kind of abnormal event within the brain such as anatomic, metabolic, o r electrophysiologic pathology; o r perhaps an attempt b y a normal child t o adapt himself defensively against an excessively stressful environment. There i s still considerable confusion and/or disagreement between different authorities relative to infantile autism and childhood schizophrenia. Some authorities indicate there i s no difference between autism and schizophrenia. Rimland (1964) has indicated a rather convincing differentiation which is represented in the following table. This should not be considered as empirically conclusive evidence to show the distinctions between childhood schizophrenia and autism, but it is a good assessment guide to aid professionals and parents to discern the major, obvious behavioral characteristics between autistic and schizophrenic children.

Table 1

Major Distinctions Between Infantile Autism and Childhood Schizophrenia

(Adapted from Rimland, B., Infantile Autism.
New York, Appleton Century Crofts, 1964)

	Infantile Autism	Childhood Schizophrenia
1. Onset and Course	Present from the beginning of life.	Disordered behavior follows an initial period of normal development.
		These children are almost always described as being the "best child the mother ever had."
2. Health and Appearance	Almost invariably in excellent health, beautiful and well formed, and usually of dark complexion.	Generally in poor health from birth. Respiratory, circulatory, metabolic, and digestive difficulties are very common.
		These children are usually thin, pale, have translucent skin, blonde hair and blue eyes.
3. EEG	Usually a normal EEG	80% of these children show abnormal EEGs.

Table 1, continued

	Infantile Autism	Childhood Schizophrenia
4. Physical Responsiveness	Autistic children typically do not adapt their bodies to their mother's or other adults when being carried or held. They are stiff and unresponsive.	These children are noted for their strong tendency to "mold" to their adults like plastic or dough.
5. Autistic Aloneness	These children are noted for failing to adjust to adults emotionally as well as posturately. They are described as being aloof.	These children are rarely called unresponsive or unappealing. They immediately capture the empathy of the adult who is often seduced into a false evaluation of treatment possibility.
6. Preservation of "Sameness of Environment"	This is a cardinal symptom.	Not at all common in schizophrenic children.
7. Hallucinations	Absence of hallucinations.	Many visual and auditory hallucinations.
8. Motor Performance	Excellent motor ability in both gross body movements and finger dexterity.	Poor coordination, locomotion, and balance.

Table 1, continued

	Autistic Children	Childhood Schizophrenia
9. Language	Absence of the words "yes" and "I." The word "I" is not used by the autistic child, until about age 7, and then only sparingly.	No difference in the use of the word "I" between these children and the control group.
10. Idiot Savant Performance	Unusual memory, musical, and mechanical performances.	Not found in this group.
11. Personal Orientation	The autistic child is described as unoriented, detached, appearing disinterested in events occurring around him. Aloof and oblivious to the environment, then in conflict with it.	These children appear to be disoriented, confused and anxious. More accessible than the autistic child.
12. Conditionability	Difficult to condition and hard to extinguish.	Easily conditioned.
13. Twins	Unusual number of monozygotic twins reported.	Not found in childhood schizophrenia.
14. Family Background	Extremely high education and intellectual background and low divorce rate among parents of these children.	71% of the homes of this group are "inadequate."
15. Familial Mental Disorders	Strikingly low incidence of mental illness.	Strong familial dependency. Much higher rate of psychosis in the ancestors of schizophrenic children.

Treatment of Autistic Children

Conventional methods o f treatment and orthodox methods of teaching have been tried and proven somewhat unsuccessful: play therapy and psychoanalysis, conditioning techniques, and intensive teaching have ended very often i n discouragement and disillusionment. The child fails to improve after endless hours of treatment. The therapist o r teacher, unable to accept this a s a failure o f his own personality or skill tends t o regard the child as unteachable a n d untreatable and t u r n s his attention t o less needy children and ignores the withdrawn autistic c h i l d. Treatment for autistic children must begin a s early as p o s s i b l e. Physical f a c t o r s m u s t also be primarily attended. T h e child-mother relationship should be improved a s much as possible, and efforts to comfort emotional problems within the family must be undertaken. Also, the parents must be aware t h a t taking the child from the home for treatment may cause further feelings of rejection and forms of withdrawal.

Mother substitutes have been quite successful treatment methods for a child who has been hospitalized. The mother substitute is slowly eliminated by the introduction and reappearance of the natural mother. A close contact must be maintained with the substitute and natural mother and child until the child is ready to leave the hospital.

Education of Autistic Children

The basic principle in training and educating autistic children is that the teacher should f i r s t t r y to e s t a b l i s h a relationship w i t h t h e child, which m a y b e accomplished b y using w h a t- ever a c t i v i t y the c h i l d w i l l undertake a s a means to bridge the gap between them. One should then try cajoling him into gradually expanding his aimless and often mechanistic activity into activity that begins to approach a purpose and eventually an educational skill.

The teacher should set her goals low enough to allow for the slow progression of the autistic child. Autistic children will have a tendency to stick to certain levels of educational tasks, but the teacher should not lose interest even though the child tends to maintain a plateau. One should discover new ways to lead them and not give up easily.

After the initial teacher-child introduction is made, the child should be gradually introduced into small groups, and put on a rudimentary program or a schedule. After a group process is established; the child's fear of the outer world may be lessened and he may have less reason to ward off reality.

The schooling for the autistic child should be a part of the normal school system. These children's basic problems are not being able to relate to others. Therefore, if they are segregated into a class consisting only of other autistic children, the milieu purpose would be defeated. A grouping of emotionally disturbed and mentally retarded children in somewhat equal numbers has some indication for a successful class situation. Parents and teachers must remain aware, though, that this child is not suddenly going to exchange his autistic behavior and become a model child. It takes time, patience, and more time.

REFERENCES

Rimland, Bernard. <u>Infantile Autism, The Syndrome and Its Implications for a Neural Theory of Behavior</u> New York: Appleton, Century, Croft, 1964.

CRIMINOLOGY: HOMICIDAL CHILDREN

Murder as a human action has been studied in depth by students of human behavior from time immemorial. However, no clearcut psychological mechanisms for killer's catastrophic behavior h a s been formulated. The dynamics of the urge to kill have not been adequately explored. People murder other people for a variety of superficial reasons. A person may commit murder at any time in life, from childhood to old age. For purposes of this discussion, any individual under sixteen years of age who commits murder is considered a child who kills.

Approximately 700 children commit murder each year. Many of these are seemingly well-behaved youngsters from good homes. One-third of the victims are members of the immediate family. It has been observed that the potential child killer is emotionally depraved and usually indifferent or antagonistic toward the opposite sex. He is fearful of social environment and has a strong preoccupation with death. He may be a compulsive arsonist. Arson may be considered one of the more obvious warning signs of hostility.

Why do children kill? A certain combination of environmental factors is required. One or more of these may be operational at the time of the murder. Primarily, the child must be extremely impulsive and have poor inhibitory control of his aggressions. The victim, in most instances, serves as a source of extreme irritation to the child, (Podolsky, 1965).

Symptoms

Bender, (1953) who has made a study of children who kill, believes that there are certain danger symptoms that should be considered significant. These are as follows:

1. Organic brain damage with an impulse disorder, an abnormal EEG and epilepsy
2. Childhood schizophrenia accompanied by pre-pseudoneurotic phase or by anti-social paranoid preoccupations in the pseudopsychopathic phase
3. Compulsive fire setting
4. Defeating school retardations (e.g. reading disability)
5. Extremely unfavorable home conditions and life experiences
6. Personal experience with violent death.

Bender (1953) somewhat indicates that any child who has been associated with such a death is dangerous thereafter.

The so-called "model" child's extreme goodness is believed to be a warning sign. Overrestrained and overpolite children are often emotionally crippled. They are unable to appreciate and return feelings of affection and love, yet they cannot vent their hostilities. In one case, a boy who became a pyromaniac at the age of four had few social contacts, played only with a white mouse, and despite high intelligence, was a poor student. In his teens

77

he shot and killed five people and displayed no remorse. During subsequent examinations, he complained that his mother was concerned only with what the neighbors thought and that his father spoke to him only during whippings. These trivialities were of greater concern to this boy than the fact that he had committed five murders, (Podolsky, 1965).

In a study of eight boys who had committed murder, Michaels (1955) found definite psychodynamic patterns in these boys and their families. Six of the eight boys had been bed wetters until they were six or seven years old and one had been persistently enuretic until his present age of sixteen. While this incidence of enuresis was not statistically significant, there was always a correlation between persistent enuresis and juvenile delinquency. Both seemed to be manifestations of a character disorder.

Michaels believes that this type of character structure (enuretic) is probably associated with a high degree of irritability, explosiveness, impulsiveness, and lack of inhibition which permeates the entire personality. In the boys previously mentioned this character structure, combined with psychodynamic factors in their background, might well have resulted in the extremely antisocial behavior that they displayed.

The death wish is strong in children who are inclined to kill. Bender (1954) suggests that there are five circumstances in which the death wish may become dangerously exaggerated. These are as follows:

1. The family rivalry situation becomes intense because of some external factor.
2. The rivalry situation occurs in a family environment that is not normal to the child such as a foster home where the positive af-

fective (love) responses are not strong enough to curb aggressive tendencies.

3. Organic factors make the child feel inferior, helpless, disorganized, and in greater need of the love of which he is deprived.

4. Educational difficulties become insurmountable in a child with enough insight to sense the inferior status into which he's being forced. These difficulties include reading disabilities in children of good intelligence who do not receive adequate help.

5. Severe aggressiveness on the part of the parents, forces the child to protect himself from them with the only reaction pattern he knows.

Children who commit murder describe their antisocial behavior in terms of changing their position of being passively vulnerable to destruction, to a position in which they are doing the destroying. These children also describe their actions in terms of doing to someone else what has been done to them.

Schizophrenic children who commit murder are often characterized by an unusual amount of uncontrolled instinctual expression. Violence, brutality, and crimes of assault appear in the family background in much greater proportion than one would anticipate in the general population, (Bender, 1954).

Parents sometimes report a history of uncontrolled rage reactions, as well as early and continued sexual experiences of many kinds. The sexual experiences seem to be repeated and varied and they may include sadism, masochism, and voyeurism. Children tend to express their conflicts by behavioral, affective, or somatic routes rather than by ideational routes. Children who develop antisocial patterns often have parents who are themselves antisocial; the child identifies with this aspect.

The child who kills is beset by fantasies of

burning up, f a l l i n g apart, or disintegrating. His
defenses are poorly structured. Outbursts of r a g e
and a n t i s o c i a l behavior are indications of this.
The child's uncontrolled b e h a v i o r at school or in
t h e neighborhood m a y bring h i m to the attention of
t h e authorities. H i s behavior may take the form of
violent temper t a n t r u m s , urinating, or defecating
i n the classroom, attacks on other children, biting
o r smashing things. There is often evidence of earlier and continued extreme violence, such as smashing
a n d destroying furniture o r violent attacks on sib-
lings. These are some of the symptoms that may lead
to murder.

T h e impulse-ridden child is often soil in which
murder m a y flourish. This type of child has a traumatic background. T h e trauma m a y occur from actual
loss of p a r e n t s by desertion o r abandonment or as
emotional withdrawal because of alcoholism or depression. Some o f these children have had numerous foster home placements and have had n o sustaining relationship w i t h any parent figure. T h e y experience
extreme anxiety, a n d to lessen this anxiety they begin to act out, (Devereaux, 1951).

Electroencephalograms o f child murderers h a v e
unusual s i x and fourteen per second peaks, according
to Woods and Stehle. They hypothesize that t h e dys-
r h y t h m i a does not, in itself induce violence, but
that it serves as a biologically determined stress on
an already impoverished ego. In t h i s repressed ego
state, primitive aggression emerges a n d is associated w i t h violent acting o u t of conflict previously
h e l d in check by the defensive system o f the e g o.
This is in contrast to epilepsy, in which the presence

80

of a seizure discharge provides a "short-cutting" mechanism with relief of tension, (Karpman, 1960).

Some illustrative cases are as follows: A twelve year old newsboy had an excellent reputation in the community. He went to the house of one of his customers to collect payment for newspapers and having received the money, was about to leave. He then turned back for no reason that he could recall. He knocked on the door and the thirty-eight year old woman came to let him in. He asked for a drink of water and stepped inside. The woman turned to get the water and as she passed it to him, he hit her on the head with a milk bottle, knocking her to the floor. She was unconscious, but apparently not dead. He slipped a laundry bag over her head, pulled up the strings and strangled her. He then stuck a knife in her abdomen. He said he had been told that a dead person would not bleed. He also wrapped a towel around her neck. He ransacked the house but took nothing.

The boy returned to a group of other boys who were playing ball and then went home. No one noticed any change in him whatsoever. Four days later the victim's daughter came home and found the body on the floor. Since the boy had been seen entering the house, he was questioned and freely admitted his guilt. He could offer no motive for the murder and none was ever discovered. He said an impulse had come over him. He pleaded guilty and was sentenced to life imprisonment.

An eleven year old boy was an only child whose parents had been divorced for a time when the mother had charged the father with cruelty and abusive treat-

ment.   Later they were remarried.   The boy did not
seek the company of other children to any great extent;
however, he sometimes engaged in aggressive wrestling.
The boy had considerable difficulty in school.   His
teacher said that his behavior was peculiar.   He
would run around the room making weird noises.   He
did not seem to know the difference between right and
wrong.   He attempted to remove other boys' trousers
and became increasingly aggressive.   He also set several fires at this time.   The boy demonstrated   some
of the early manifestations of childhood schizophrenia.
The symptoms included problems in relating to his
peers, bizarre behavior, withdrawn tendencies,   flat-
ness of affect, lack of remorse or guilt for antiso -
cial behavior, rage and explosive murderous violence.
The boy suddenly murdered a playmate.

A fourteen year old boy had an excellent reputation in his neighborhood, his mother was psychotic and
he lived with relatives.   He was a junior high school
student and there was nothing in his record to suggest any behavioral disturbance.   For some time he
had been "going steady" and had kissed on several occasions, but there had been no overt sexual experience.
One day the boy and girl rode to a ballgame on his
bicycle.   She was scantily dressed and sat facing him
on the handlebars.   They started home in the early
evening.   After going a short way, they stopped at a
park.   The girl dismounted but the boy remained sitting on the bicycle.   He then drew a pistol from his
pocket and showed it to her. (He had been carrying the
gun around for some time and had fired it at   least
once.)   When she said, "Don't shoot me,"   he pulled
the trigger four times.   The bullets passed through

her chest, killing her instantly. The boy rode away for a while, then came back and gave himself up. Although every possible theory was explored, no motive for the murder was ever found. The boy said he did not know why he did it. It was an impulse. He pleaded guilty to second-degree murder and received a life sentence. There were no conduct infractions during his years in prison and no psychotic process was discovered.

Items on childhood murders appear in the newspapers almost every week. A fourteen year old boy shot a high school teacher because he had been reprimanded for failure to complete a school assignment. A sudden urge to kill someone was advanced as another fourteen year old boy's reason for stabbing a thirteen year old cousin. Angered because he was denied the use of the family car, a fifteen year old boy killed his father with a rifle. An eleven year old boy shot his parents and a brother because he had been spanked. Many more such cases could be cited.

All the factors that contribute to childhood murders are not known at the present time. The murder may be motivated by some well-founded reason, an obscure reason, or no reason at all. A great deal of research remains to be done, (Podolsky, 1965).

In conclusion it may be said that some of the reasons for childhood murders may be associated with brain damage, childhood schizophrenia, compulsive setting of fires, marked school retardation, unfavorable home conditions, and life experiences or personal experience with violent death. Brutality and crimes of assault often appear in the family backgrounds of schizophrenic children who commit murder. In many childhood murders, motives are lacking. It is not too uncommon to read t h e newspaper and see a report, "G o o d boy kills parents or teacher. He w a s a star athlete. He was a member of the Student Senate. He was an honor student." Somewhere along t h e life habits of this child, he surely emitted clues about h i s bewildered world, but we as parents and teachers failed to screen them. Of course, if we were to predict tomorrow's behavior based on past performance, we w o u l d probably say that the star athlete, good student, etc., would continue expressing good behavior. We w o u l d miss, though, on many kids , because they e v i d e n t l y cry for help in such subtle, indirect ways that their calls fail to be recognized, and then--MURDER.

REFERENCES

Bender, L auretta, A Dynamic Psychopathology o f Childhood. Springfield, Illinois: Charles C. Thomas, 1954.

_____, Aggression, Hostility and Anxiety in Children. Springfield, Illinois: Charles C. Thomas, 1953.

Devereaux, G., "Neurotic Crime vs. Criminal Behavior," Psychiatric Quarterly, 25, (January, 1951).

Karpman, B., "T h e Principles and A i m s of Crimin a l Psychopathology," Journal of Criminal Psychopathology, (January, 1960).

Michaels, Joseph, J., Disorders of Character. C h a r l e s C. Thomas, 1955.

Podolsky, Edward, "Children Who Kill," Journal of General Practice.

DRUGS

The phenomenon of d r u g s is o n e which involves many abstractions of feelings and a c t i o n s for both t h e parents and c h i l d r e n . Parents will deny the possibility that their child could ever involve h i m- s e l f in the drug scene. The kids may wonder why or h o w their parents can remain s o ignorant t o the i r drug habits. T h e kids, may actually consciously, or unconsciously, be wondering why the p a r e n t s d on't care. "I f they really cared, they would be aware of my troubles and help m e ." Consequently, the sons and daughters continue the d r u g activity until they get caught by t h e law, or have a bad trip and are hospi- talized.

Parents, teachers, be aware of the kids' actions. Do you see sudden o r gradual changes in their manner of d r e s s? Is their behavior radical, illogical, or unassuming? Do they wear sunglasses in t h e house or classrooms and m a k e excuses f o r their needs? Does their speech change? Does their physical coordination change? Do you see anything t h a t is not consistent with the students' past normal activity?

These kids m a y become very sophisticated in the d r u g scene. They do not n e e d the illegal traffic drugs. T h e s e kids c a n find over-the-counter drugs

without prescriptions t h a t will effect a h i g h . I
have worked with kids who have used cold pills, cough
s y r u p, asthma medicine, motion sickness pills, food
extracts, etc.; a n d if taken without regard f o r the
consequences, these counter drugs can be very danger-
o u s. Recently, I was working with two teenage girls
who had taken motion sickness pills, aspirin, and coke.
After pumping both stomachs, one girl still n e a r l y
died. The other girl's face was so swollen she could
not open her eyes.

I've seen these kids so tuned-in to drug effects
that they were a b l e to take t i m e -lapse cold pills,
empty the clear capsule, sort o u t the little colored
beads into groups of different colors, a n d then take
e n o u g h of certain colors to get high. I've worked
with kids who have taken asthma medicine, wrapped i t
in t i s s u e paper and swallowed it with coke. A boy
who did this then stood a r o u n d barking like a dog.
He was not visually perceiving objects with s p a t i a l
relationship. T h e bathroom s i n k was on t h e floor
rather than on the wall and he would talk to the sink
on the floor.

There seems to be no limit to the search for effective highs. T h e y have sniffed gasoline, g l u e ,
p a i n t thinner, butane lighter fluid, lighter fluid,
and s p r a y cans. Of course some kids don't start on
the over-the-counter d r u g s. They s t a r t on grass,
L.S.D., etc., but regardless t h e y may all reach the
same end of the road.

Education is the key to s o l v i n g this problem.
It is m u c h too late to wait until the kid is hooked
and t h e n ask him why. He can't a n s w e r you. He
doesn't k n o w why or how he got started. He c a n ' t
s p e a k meaningfully; he will need e x c u s e s for his

behavior, not a change of behavior. Consequently this kid is a very difficult person with whom to counsel. Be aware, parents and teachers, these kids will give us clues to their behavior, but we must tune in rather than screen out their changes of behavior. Don't hit the panic button, but do remain alert.

Don't try to talk with the kids about physical or emotional long term effects of L.S.D., marijuana, speed, etc., because they can probably very cleverly and logically tell you that it is no more harmful than smoking or drinking. I believe your best rationale is one in which you approach the legal aspects, because they will not accept a moralizing lesson. Tell the kids, "Okay, I don't know the short or long term effects of drugs. Maybe, they are harmless, I don't know; but I do know that it is many years in jail if you are caught, and that should be our concern, not how right or wrong, good or bad; but that drugs can, through legal aspects, get you many years in jail and ruin your life."

Try to get an understanding that you are not turning against them--the kids, and you are not screening out their lives and image, but you are trying to preserve an interest in them and that you really care. Don't say, "I knew you would end up on drugs, you always were stupid."

The following case study is a good example of the development of drug usage and the ultimate consequences:

A white unmarried female of 19 years of age who comes from a broken home, her mother is an alcoholic and her father, whom she seldom saw, is a small rancher. The first memories she has of her mother is of her crying desperately every night for an answer to save her marriage. Another memory is of her mother leaving her in a car at Christmas time in front of a hotel for three days and two nights. This happened when she was five years old. Finally, after three days, she left the car and went into the hotel to look for her mother. She knocked on every door and finally found her mother in bed with another man. After this experience, she went to live with her father in another state. She has not seen her mother since that experience.

She has one older brother 21 years of age. Her father was always partial to his son and left her alone most of the time. The only time he paid attention to her was when he wanted her to do some work.

When she was 12, they moved to another state and her father remarried. Her step-mother had two children of her own, ages 16 and 12. There was considerable rivalry between the children. Her step-mother constantly mistreated her and her brother. She stated that her step-mother used to beat her unmercifully. She had to do all the housework and when her father would come home, he would ask her what she had done that day. Her step-mother used to tell her to go outside and play, and she would then tell the father that she, the step-mother, had worked so hard all day and that she had been a "brat" and had not done a thing. Naturally, she would get into trouble. After several years of marriage, her step-mother had a baby boy. She was now a built in babysitter. To illustrate how cruel the step mother was to her children and to her brother, she told of an incident which to her, at the time, was terrifying. Her little brother was four years old at the time of the incident. He took a pistol out of the desk drawer one afternoon and shot his mother in the back. She was not seriously wounded, but I think this information shows the home life this girl had.

As the home problems began to mount, she began to seek new friends and an escape from her problems. This is the time she began to take drugs moderately. The first time she experimented with drugs was when she was in the 9th grade. She was living in another state with her father and step-mother at this time. The first drug she experimented with was marijuana. She smoked this with two of her girlfriends. The first time she smoked pot she did not really have any effects from it. She began smoking every day. She and her two friends would leave school and go to one of their homes and smoke while their parents were at work. The first effects she remembers are feelings of being scared, laughing a lot, being ashamed and praying.

She smoked pot two years before trying any harder drugs. She states that when she smokes pot, she has to be the center of attention. She laughs a lot and especially enjoys listening to music. If she is not the center of attention, she withdraws. She also states she is terribly hungry after smoking marijuana. Her reason for drug taking was to escape from the loneliness she experienced. She only smokes when she is with a group of people.

When she was 16, she met a boy and she fell in love with him. The boy became a father figure to her as he would not allow her to smoke marijuana or take any other drugs. She spent a lot of time with the boy and his parents. She more or less lived with them. Shortly after her 16th birthday they became engaged. The engagement lasted for a year and a half. After the boy broke the engagement, she went to pieces. She was terribly lonely. This is when she began taking drugs extensively. She also began to see a psychiatrist at this time. This was her junior year in high school.

She then turned to mescaline. She stated that mescaline made her have body rushes and this made her feel like a woman. Her behavior was amusing to her and she recalls that all the colors she saw were in pastels. She used mescaline every day for a month and a half. At the end of her junior year in high school she dropped out of school. She states that her behavior in class was very bad. She was very belligerent in class, and she states that she just was not interested in anything, especially in school.

After this, she moved back to her home state with her father and brother. Her father had found out about her drug taking and wanted to get her away from the drugs and from the friends she had. However, upon her return home, she tried acid. She stated at one point that she used it daily and then tapered off for about a month. When she started using it again, she had a very frightening experience with acid. The trip goes as follows: "People were dripping out of trees. Then I looked at myself and I became different parts of my body. People had very distorted faces. People kept coming out of the walls. I looked at my hands and all I could see were my bones. I was at a party when this happened, and I went back into the bedroom by myself. I was so scared. Then

90

I saw myself burning in hell. Later I talked to God; I actually saw his face and I talked to him. I began to yell and scream to God that if he would only get me out of there I would dedicate my life to helping others. Then I began to scream for someone to take me to the hospital. Several of the kids came in, and they decided to take me to another house where I could be by myself and could let the drug wear off." This was her last trip on L.S.D., and this was ten months ago.

She stated that while in highschool, she went to several school counselors concerning her lack of interest and her behavior in school. She stated that the counselor would ask her questions, then she would make up some fantastically wild story so that it would appear that she was beyond their help. She has also seen several psychiatrists but she has never told them any truthful things about her or her life.

She did finish high school by taking correspondence courses while she was living at home. She is now living in a large city with several girls. She has been to see a psychohogist, but after five sessions, she terminated herself. The psychologist believes she is a borderline schizophrenic girl. Part of this schizophrenia could be because of her drug taking, but he is not certain since he only saw her a total of five sessions.

Since she moved to the city nine months ago, she has completely changed her life style. Shortly after she moved, she met a college student who soon became another parent figure to her. He took care of her and she was happy and stopped most of her drug taking. However, this new guy did allow her to smoke pot, because he enjoyed smoking it too. At this time she a l s o began experimenting with sex. Sex became security to her. Sex m a d e boys respond to her, and their response made her feel loved. She was no long- er lonely. She confused sex w i t h love. The r e l a - tionship lasted several months.

Next, s h e met another young man. Her relation- ship with him lasted for the several months that s h e lived with him, although it was strictly sex oriented. During these months she only smoked marijuana several times. He did not like for her to smoke; therefore, she didn't unless they had a fight and then she would smoke just to make him angry. This relationship soon ended and she fell back upon drugs. This was only two months ago. As you can see by now a pattern has d e - veloped. As long as she has a mother figure, s h e no longer needs drugs, but as soon as she loses a moth- er figure, she resorts to drug taking.

Her drug taking started because o f h e r loneli- ness and her bad home life. She is basically a strong person because she has stopped taking most drugs that she relied upon heavily. She has come a long way, but at any time, if with the wrong group of people and if she is lonely, she could be convinced t o use d r u g s extensively again.

The following table may be of value to you as in- terested parents and teachers to help evaluate and/or identify a youngster's change of behavior.

Table 2

NARCOTIC	POSSIBLE BEHAVIOR SYMPTOMS	MATERIAL EVIDENCE	PHYSICAL--EMOTIONAL CONSEQUENCES
Glue Sniffing	Violence, drunk appearance; dreamy or blank expression.	Tubes of glue; glue smears; large paper bags or handkerchiefs.	Lung/Brain/Liver damage; death through suffocation or choking; anemia.
Heroin (H., Horse, Scat, Junk, Snow, Stuff, Harry, Joy Powder) Morphine (White stuff, Miss Emma, M., Dreamer) Codeine (School-boy)	Stupor/drowsiness; needle marks on body; watery eyes; loss of appetite; blood stain on shirt sleeve; running nose.	Needle or hypodermic syringe; cotton; tourniquet string; rope; belt; burnt bottle; caps or spoons; glassine envelopes.	Death from overdose; mental deterioration destruction of brain and liver; Hepatitis; embolisms.
Cough Medicine containing codein and opium	Drunk appearance; lack of coordination; confusion; excessive itching.	Empty bottles of cough medicine.	Causes addiction.
Marijuana (Pot; Grass, Locoweed, Mary Jane, Hashish; Tea; Gage; Reefers)	Sleepiness; wandering mind; enlarged eye pupils; lack of coordination; craving for sweets; increased appetite.	Strong odor of burnt leaves; small seeds in pocket lining; cigarette paper; discolored fingers.	Inducement to take stronger narcotics.

93

Table 2, continued

NARCOTIC	POSSIBLE BEHAVIOR SYMPTOMS	MATERIAL EVIDENCE	PHYSICAL--EMOTIONAL CONSEQUENCES
LSD (Acid, Sugar, Big D, Cubes, Trips) DMT (Businessman's High) STP	Severe hallucinations; feelings of detachment; incoherent speech; cold hands and feet; vomiting; laughing and crying.	Cube sugar with discoloration in center; strong body odor; small tube of liquid.	Suicidal tendencies; unpredictable behavior; chronic exposure causes brain damage. LSD causes chromosomal breakdown in many instances.
Amphetamines (Bennies, Dexies, Co-Pilots, Wake-ups, Lid Poppers, Hearts, Pep Pills) Methamphetamines (Speed; Dynamite)	Aggressive behavior; giggling; silliness; rapid speech; confused thinking; no appetite; extreme fatigue; dry mouth; shakiness.	Jars of pills of varying colors; chain smoking.	Death from overdose; hallucinations, Methamphetamines sometimes cause temporary psychosis.
Barbiturates (Barbs; Blue Devils; Candy; Yellow Jackets; Phennies; Blue Heavens; Goof Balls; Downs)	Drowsiness; stupor; dullness; slurred speech; drunk appearance; vomiting.	Pills of varying colors.	Death from overdose, or causes of addiction, convulsions and death as a result of withdrawal.

94

Reference: I. Taxel, Woodmere, New York, 1970.

ENURESIS AND ENCOPRESIS

Most children are toilet trained by the age of three, but an ample margin for error is allowed and urinary incontinence usually is not labeled enuresis until after the age of four. In most instances, enuresis occurs only at night during sleep, but diurnal enuresis also is seen, (Chapman, 1967).

Enuresis is involuntary urination during sleep mainly, and commonly referred to as "bed wetting" or "Nocturnal enuresis." The term is actually inclusive of lapses of urinary control in the waking state, "diurnal enuresis," but this is rarely seen, (Coville, Costello, and Roeke, 1960).

Nocturnal enuresis is one of the most common symptoms of emotional problems of childhood. Some

authorities e s t i m a t e that in only five percent of
incontinence, t h e symptom is caused by physical factors such a s bladder infections, diabetes, epilepsy,
or genitourinary anomalies, (Wolman, 1965). Crosby
(cited in Yates, 1970), d e f i n e d essential enuresis
as follows: (1) "The involuntary a n d unconscious
passing o f urine after an a r b i t r a r y age limit of
three years, in the a b s e n c e of significant congenital or a c q u i r e d defect or disease of the nervous
a n d uro-genital systems, a n d in the absence of significant psychological defects." Michaels (cited in
Yates, 1970), defined enuresis as follows: (2) "Uncontrolled, unintentional v o i d i n g of urine at o n e
expulsion usually occurring during sleep; i t may be
considered to be present if bedwetting o c c u r s past
the age of three, a liberal time for control of urination to h a v e been established in so-called normal
individuals.

Some authors divided enuresis into several categories (W o l m a n , 1965): (1) Revenge enuresis, a n
unconscious expression of rebellion a g a i n s t strict
parental demands. (2) Regressive enuresis, a psych-
osexual regression as the r e s u l t of some emotional
threat. M o r e than half of enuretic children have a
c o n f u s e d sexual identification and they dream o f
urination i n the position of the opposite s e x. (3)
Enuresis with castration fears: Some children become
enuretic after i n j u r y , surgery, illness, or sexual
trauma. They become convinced that they have incurred
permanent damage to t h e i r genitals. (4) Enuresis
because of hysterical identification w i t h an incon-
tinent parent. (5) Enuresis b e c a u s e of lack o f
training. In s o m e large families, especially of the

96

lower socioeconomic c l a s s e s, it is accepted as the normal p a t t e rn of the family to wet the bed. T h e younger children, i f not instructed to the contrary, will continue in the family tradition.

Coville, Costello, and Rouke (1960), stated that in the 90 percent of the cases in which psychological factors were important, they found that enuresis w a s the result of e x c e s s i v e emotional tension and was usually part of a syndrome which often included nail-biting, thumb-sucking, and temper tantrums. A circular type of reaction has been observed in which the bedwetting leads to feelings of s h a m e or guilt, and these in turn i n t e n s i f y anxiety and tension, thus precipitating further bedwetting. A variety of psychodynamic i n t e r p r e t a t i o n s of enuresis have been offered. Some of these are as follows:

1. A specific expression of generalized anxiety.
2. A displacement of sexual satisfaction f r e-quently associated with r e p r e s s e d sexual fantasies.
3. An expression of hostility toward parents or as a release of aggression.
4. A persistence of immature attention-g e tt ing behavior patterns.
5. Inadequate habit training with attitudes o f indifference and apathy on the p a r t of the parents.

T h e age of the e n u r e ti c child is somewhat an artificial consideration, b e c a u s e the symptom has usually persisted from early childhood. There is no indication that intelligence is a r e l a t e d factor. Sex is, however, because m o s t reports indicate that enuresis is about twice as f r e q u e n t in boys as in g i r l s. Cultural factor studies are not sufficient, but it is probably that bed-wetting i s more accepted and therefore l e s s frequently reported in the lower classes. This e v i d e n c e , though, would be an easy

97

fact to verify o r refute in a survey of school chil-
d r e n of differing b a c k g r o u n d s, (Kessler, 1966).
Psychodynamic formulations run a gamut from h i g h l y
specific, to v e r y general conceptualizations of the
enuresis symptomatic nature, and t h e r e is agreement
among some authorities that enuresis i s a symptom of
some underlying disturbance of a fundamentally m o r e
important nature, (Yates, 1970).

Another formulation which is worth mentioning is
t h e behavioristic approach whose essence to the etiology of enuresis may be stated m o s t helpfully by a
series of propositions, (Yates, 1970).

1. That, in the newborn child, t h e voiding reflex is an extremely powerful n a t u r a l reflex and t h a t this is essential if the infant is to survive.

2. That the problem faced b y the growing child
   is to develop the h i g h e r nervous centers,
   b y both maturation and learning, to the extent that i n h i b i t o r y factors are strong
   enough to hold in check the natural r e f l e x
   until v o l u n t a r y voiding can be achieved.

3. That this a c h i v e m e n t represents a high
   level s k i l l of considerable complexity and
   that it is not, therefore, surprising t h a t
   s o m e children have difficulty in achieving
   such control (indeed, it may be argued that
   t h e really surprising fact is not that some
   children fail to achieve such control, b u t
   that most children do achieve it).

The problem to be solved t h e r e f o r e, asks the
question: H o w is n o r m a l micturitional control established; both nocturnal and diurnal, and w h a t fac-

tors are involved in the failure to achieve such control? According to Yates (1970), it is necessary to examine two aspects of micturitional control: first, the physiological processes involved; and secondly, the part played by learning.

A. Physiological Basis of Micturitional control: The physiology of normal reflex micturition is extremely complex. Briefly, urine passes from the kidneys through the ureters (by peristaltic action) into the bladder. The wall of the bladder contains the detrusor muscle which does not respond linearly to increased volume of urine, but maintains a steady level of pressure until the volume exceeds about 200 mil. Above this point, the detrusor muscle is less successful in maintaining tone (detrusor muscle tone is controlled by the antagonistic action of the pelvic and hypogastric), and begins to contract rhythmically, leading ultimately to the micturition reflex, which involves strong contractions of the detrusor muscle and relaxation of the internal followed by the external sphincters, and involuntary voiding of urine. The micturition reflex is, in fact, made up of the coordinated sequential "firing" of several simple reflexes.

B. Development of cortical control of micturition: The child faces a major task in developing voluntary control over what is a powerful and complex natural reflex. For this reason, there are several aspects of this problem which should be kept quite

seperate. First, the child must acquire
the skill of inducing voluntary urination
when the act is required to be performed,
and further, he must be able to do this
when there is low volume and pressure of
urine in the bladder. Secondly, even more
important than cortical control of the act
itself, is development of the capacity to
inhibit detrusor activity with increasing
volumes and pressures of urine, to the point
at which reflex voiding is unlikely to take
place even when the bladder is full and the
urgency to micturate is very great. At
this point very little is known except that
it seems clear that high-level inhibitory
controlling centers must be gradually established. Thirdly, having established
control of the act itself, and having developed the capacity to delay initiation of
the conditioned sequences leading to micturition; the child must also acquire the ability to exercise this control during sleep.
This can be achieved in two ways. First
the child must transfer the daytime inhibitory control to sleep; secondly, if bladder
pressures increase during sleep to the
point at which reflex voiding becomes emi-
nent, the bladder pressures must be capable
of waking the child before the reflex is
triggered and automatic voiding occurs. Finally, the child must learn to attach situational cues to the whole micturitional
sequence, so that the need to micturate will
be suggested not only by internal sensations

but also by external factors. Thus it may be concluded that successful control of urination is both a function of the acquisition of control of the mechanics of the act itself and the learning of situational cues which enable the child to anticipate needs, (Yates, 1970).

Behavior Therapy relative to Enuresis should also be examined. After enuresis is firmly established; it is a habit, and because of this, it is often treated by a conditioned response therapy. Such retraining concentrates on the cessation of the symptom. Enuresis is a special kind of symptom, it contains the potential for further emotional conflicts. A psychologically harmless cure would, therefore, be welcomed by many doctors, (Kessler, 1966).

Mowrer and Mowrer used observations from pediatric hospital situations. As early as 1909, an electrical pad was devised which, when moistened, closed a circuit and rang a bell. A nurse came, and changed the child. Under these conditions, it was reported that a number of children no longer wet their beds. Mowrer and Mowrer improved this device and added a number of important therapeutic elements, (Ullman and Krasner, 1969).

Another refinement, which points to the improvement of technology within behavioral principles, was also presented by Lovibond in 1963 and 1964. Lovibond noted that the behavior to be changed is the contraction of the detrusor and relaxation of the sphincter muscles. Lovibond's Twin Signal Apparatus was therefore, designed with a loud, disruptive "Hooter," which startles the person and leads to a reflexive tightening of the spincter m u s c l e . This "Hooter" stops r a p i d l y, so that tightening of the muscle is followed in t i m e by the cessation of the unpleasant n o i s e . A softer, gentler buzzer t h e n awakens an attendant (parent) who takes the child to the bathroom to complete the appropriate b e h a v i o r . Lovibond's analysis fits the general sociopsychological paradigm that the goal of therapy is an acceptable response to a situation rather than solely t h e elimination of an objectionable response, (Ullmann and Krasner, 1969).

When the conditioned response method works; it generally does so i n fairly short order; a matter of weeks, or at most, months. Some children d o not respond; for these children, bed-wetting may be serving a special purpose w h i c h is not easily relinquished. T o discover the purpose and alter t h e behavior then requires individual psychotherapy. The psychodynamics approach describes that the enuresis e x p r e s s e s an unconscious wish, one which is repressed because o f the anxiety or guilt associated with it. There probably is no way of establishing the fact, but it seems to some authors t h a t when the unconscious w i s h is strong, a learning approach will fail. When the conditioned response method works, it seems l o g i c a l to assume that enuresis w a s the result of faulty t r a i n - ing, or that the precipitating psychological conflict wore itself out, leaving only the habit. Enuresis may have a simple beginning, as in jealousy of a new baby, but it is a symptom which often picks up new meanings as the child grows. The m o r e remote the onset, the more complicated the treatment process, (Kessler, 1966).

Encopresis

The term encopresis was introduced in 1926. One

of the f i r s t reports in the American literature was
made by Hale Shirley in 1938. He reported that almost
three percent o f the children referred to the psychiatric clinic of the Harriet Lane Home, in Baltimore,
had encopresis, and the b o y s outnumbered the girls
five to one.   There have been few subsequent reports
a n d these are mostly t r e a t m e n t reports of single
cases.   Virtually nothing is known about prevalence,
epidemiology, o r the history of u n t r e a t e d cases,
(Kessler, 1966).

Kanner (cited in Yates, 1970), defines e ncopresis
as an a c t of involuntary defecation which is not di-
r e c t l y caused by organic illness. To Yates t h i s
definition i s not entirely satisfactory and he cites
additional information provided by W a r s o n et. al.,
who defined encopresis as a disturbance in regulation
of bowel evacuation.

Wright a n d Smith, (1971) mentioned in their report that the utilization of t e r m s connected w i t h
disorders of defecation v a r i e s , even with the same
professional discipline.   For purposes of clarifica-
tion they provided the following d e f i n i t i o n s (in
Wright and Smith, 1971):

Constipation -- is the clinical symptom o f i n-
frequent evacuation o f stool, difficult e v a c -
uation, o r the evacuation of s m a l l amounts of
s t o o l sometimes of an abnormally hard consistency.

Megacolon -- is the dilation o f the rectum a n d
or colon by retained stool. The term   implies a
progressive retention of stool.   T h e differen-
tial etiologies of megacolon are discussed, too,
but it is to be noted that in one sense, all instances of megacolon represent a secondary re-

103

sponse or result from a primary rectal or colon-
ic obstruction.

Encopresis -- is the voluntary o r involuntary
passage of a stool, or a distinct bowel movement
with soiling of clothes.

Soiling --is a constant, apparently involuntary,
seepage of feces.

Hirshsprung's Disease -- is a congenital agang -
lionic megacolon in which megacolon of a portion
o r all of the large intestine develops as a result of the absence of normal innervation in the
wall of the rectum and colon.

Mo s t children who soil beyond the age of three,
or four, suffer f r o m emotional rather than physical
problems. This problem is common among pre-schoolers,
but it is also found among school-age children.   The
older the child the more serious the pathology.   The
symptom itself is v e r y annoying to parents.   Their
criticism and shaming of the c h i l d usually lead him
to hide his soiled underwear, w h i c h brings further
deterioration in the parent-child r e l a t i o n s h i p .
Encopresis may serve as a form o f revenge, as a continuous r e b e l l i o n against strict toilet training,
and against parental authority in general.   The symptom then represents a symbolic expression of the con -
flicts with parents,   (Wolman, 1965).

Emotionally caused encopresis is much less common than enuresis, but it is occasionally encountered
in clinical practice.   It m a y develop when t o i l e t
training deteriorates into a p r o l o n g e d battle between mother and child.   In very passive c h i l d r e n
encopresis may be a s y m p t o m through which they unconsciously e x p r e s s resentment toward domineering,

104

harsh parents. It also may occur in children whose mothers worry obsessively about bowel movements and deluge the child with enemas and catharsics to "regulate" the child's bowel movements, (Chapman, 1967).

Psychoanalytic writers, since Freud, have placed some attention on the anal developmental stage (in which the child progresses from initial autoerotic pleasurable elimination to the anal retentive and anal sadistic states, etc.), particularly in its supposed relationship to later personality traits (e.g., obsessive-complusive behavior). Sterba (1949) related encopresis to fears of castration. Burns (1941) and Pinkerton (1958) considered encopresis to be a form of aggression against a hostile, threatening environment. One of the most systematic developments of the psychodynamic viewpoint, however, is that of Warson et. al., (1954). They determined (largely on a single intensive case study) that the problem was a mutually enjoyable somatic relation - ship between the mother and the child in infancy; traumatic separation experiences during the transition stage between oral and anal organizations; and neurotic use of the child by the mother to express resentments, receive gratifications, etc. (Yates, 1970).

Sometimes patients not only present a history of infrequent stooling, but also present a history of diarrhea or constant seepage. Generally, soiling is caused by an acquired or psychogenic megacolon, (Wright and Smith, 1971). Wright and Smith indicate that the time of the onset of the symptomatology is usually neonatal with the organic aganglionic megacolon, and more characteristically at the time of toilet training or later in the case of acquired megacolon. A past history of obstruction requiring hospitalization is more frequent in the patient with congenital organic megacolon. When bright blood passes with the stool or there exists difficult defecation with pain; it is an indication of anal fissures and secondarily acquired megacolon.

Wright and Smith (1971) further stated that medical examination of the child with a megacolon will show a distended abdomen. At times a massively dilated loop of colon can be seen through the thin abdominal wall. Masses of fecal material can often be seen or felt. Examination of the anal region will show the presence or absence of soiling, or the presence of an anal fissure. By contrast, in the case of congenital aganglionic megacolon the rectum is usually empty; rarely is there evidence of soiling.

Wright and Smith also expressed that if one understands the nature of the megacolon, it is possible to realize how an encopretic symptom could continue after disappearance of the psychological problem which may have caused the symptom in the first place. If the child has a psychological problem which causes him to retain fecal material, he may develop megacolon and soiling. If the psychological problem which caused the child to retain feces is eradicated, the symptoms of soiling can still continue; because the distended colon cannot respond by contracting to the stimulation of pressure provided by normal amounts of fecal material. Feces are thus retained (though not for psychogenic reasons); the colon remains impacted, and soiling continues. This phenomenon has implications for the controversy

106

within p s y c h o l o g y concerning the advisability of treating symptoms (as o p p o s e d to attempting to get at the c a u s e of a psychological difficulty).   T h e fact that encopretic behavior c a n continue after the psychogenic factors responsible f o r the interaction of such behavior have disappeared, is one example from the field of pediatric psychology which supports t h e value of symptomatic treatment.

T h e application of systematic retraining sched-ules, u s i n g operant conditioning techniques, i s   a r e l a t i v e l y recent development;   a n d the results obtained must naturally be viewed with much more cau-t i o n than is the case with onuresis,   (Yates, 1970). The first important contribution was made by Neale in 1963. He stressed the retentive aspect o f encopre-sis, and considered that the initiation of the reflex was disrupted by fear following punishment.   Neale's t e c h n i q u e involved primarily the use o f a graded s e r i e s of reward-training for e x p u l s i o n at the appropriate time, in the right place, (Yates, 1970).

Gelber and Meyer in 1965, used operant condition-ing techniques to t r e a t successfully, long-standing encopresis in a boy of 14, who h a d a continuous type of encopresis, and had b e e n encopretic since birth. They stressed particularly the n e e d for discovering an appropriate reward, w h i c h may well b e different for each child, (Yates, 1970).

REFERENCES

Coville, Walter; Costello, Timothy; Rouke, Fabian; Abnormal Psychology, Barnes and Noble, 1960.

Kessler, Jane, Psychopathology of Childhood, Prentice Hall, 1966.

Thalassimos, Pablo A., Pisc. Edificio Banco de Bogota, Panama City, Panama. Personal reference.

Ullmann, L. and Krasner, L. A Psychological Approach to Abnormal Behavior, Prentice Hall, 1969.

Wolman, Benjamin, Handbook of Clinical Psychology, McGraw Hill, 1965.

Wright, Logan and Smith E. Ide, The Psychological Management of the Patient With Acquired Megacolon, Paper presented at the 2nd Annual Meeting, American Pediatric Surgical Association, Bermuda, April, 1971.

Yates, Aurbey, Behavior Therapy, John Wiles and Sons, 1970.

To many, the word "epileptic" brings to mind the picture of a h e l p l e s s , writhing creature, w h o is mentally handicapped and somewhat mentally ill; one, who cannot be helped and must be avoided least he contaminate the onlooker.   I n actuality, a convulsive seizure is not pleasant to watch.   During this brief s e i z u r e time the individual is helpless, but there the accuracy of the description ends.

Epilepsy is an a c t i v i t y manifestation of a n excessive discharge of energy in an injured p a r t of the b r a i n. The symptoms will differ depending from where the discharge occurs and how it spreads.   Epilepsy is the symptom of s o m e disorder in the brain. The n e u r o n s of the brain become overactive and fire irregularly.   T h e disturbance spreads and a seizure results;   therefore, a seizure is a sign of an unusual release of energy within the brain.

Seizures are of several types and severity. They can be so mild they are not n o t i c e d,   or so severe that they threaten life. R e s e a r c h has identified s i x t e e n patterns of seizures.   In this discussion, I will deal with the four main groups.

Grand Mal Seizures

Grand Mal seizures are quite severe a n d affect the entire appearance a n d actions of a n individual. The muscles become rigid, the eyes roll back, and the person may fall to the ground.   The rigidity g i v e s way to rhythmic jerks of the muscles. Control of the bladder may be lost. S a l i v a may flow freely which gives the appearance of f o a m around the mouth. The attacks are self-limited and usually last only one to three minutes. When an attack has subsided, the person will probably manifest a post-ictal state of fatigue and no memory of the seizure. Grand mal seizures are somewhat more common than other types of epileptic seizures and because of their nature, they are noticed often and reported frequently. All seizures will vary greatly in frequency. A child may have daily, weekly, or monthly seizures or he may have an absence of activity for years.

Petit Mal Seizure

The petit mal seizure is a blackout of consciousness, accompanied by a blank stare or a vacant look. A person may be talking calmly; he stops in the middle of a sentence, or stares vacantly, blinks and procedes without confusion or loss of continuity of speech. Another form of petit mal seizure causes the muscles to go limp. This is somewhat unusual; but a child may simply drop his pencil, or book, and again continue his task without loss of continuity. Petit mal attacks last from approximately five to twenty seconds. The person is unaware that anything occurred during that time. A child is often accused of inattention or daydreaming.

Petit mal epilepsy is primarily a symptom of children. There seems to be an age factor which enables about eighty percent of these children to "outgrow" epilepsy.

Psychomotor Seizures

This is the most difficult form of epilepsy to recognize. The seizure acts on the mental process as well as the muscles. It is sometimes described as a

brief period of automatic behavior. Psychomotor
epilepsy is also commonly known as temporal lobe
epilepsy, which is in reference to the brain area in
which the neuron disturbance lies. There is a para-
dox during a psychomotor seizure, because the person
appears to lose consciousness, yet activity appears
to be conscious. These attacks usually last only a
few seconds or minutes; but in very rare cases they
may last for longer periods of time, and the person
may perform either routine tasks, or some unusual or
antisocial act. Many times poor behavior is attributed to the individual. He has no control over these
episodes and remembers nothing or little of them.
There appears to be evidence to support an observational pattern for psychomotor epilepsy to be an adult
handicap, whereas petit mal epilepsy is primarily
found in children.

Jacksonian Seizures

Jacksonian seizures seem to be somewhat more
confined to the adult population. In Jacksonian con-
vulsions, the attacks begin in the hands or in a local
region of the body. Twitching of the muscles increases until the whole body is involved and consciousness
is lost.

This obviously is a neuron disturbance and has
a focal involvement in the brain areas controlling
particular movements. It is a modified grand mal
attack with the individual remaining conscious during
the initial spasms, but in some situations the activity may progress into a full-scale grand mal seizure.

Aura

It is estimated that for at least half of the

epileptics, there is a warning or aura. Aura is the
Latin word for wind. An aura may be something that
the person can't describe, but he knows there is a
warning of an oncoming seizure.

Etiology of Epilepsy

The exact cause of epilepsy many times is unknown.
Probable causes have been found in approximately fifty percent of the cases studied. However, the causation in one case may not be the causation in another.
Any lesion of the brain may cause epilepsy. The two
broad etiological categories which apply t o epilepsy
are referred to as idiopathic causes and symptomatic
causes. Idiopathic causes are those which are present
at b i r t h. Inheritance theories generally have been
discredited e x c e p t to the extent that an inherited
predisposition or tendency may oe present.

Symptomatic causes of epilepsy originate in many
ways. Injury or l e s i o n s to the brain may prod u c e
epilepsy. Infections, t u m o r s , lack of oxygen, o r
impaired circulation are s o m e of the injuries possible. In most cases no clear precipitating c a u s e
can be found. Brain wave patterns may indicate that
approximately o n e out of every ten p e r s o n s has a
predisposition to s e i z u r e s , but the precipitating
causes may not be known.

The Prognosis of Epilepsy

To f i n d out whether a person has seizures, and
what kind, and what may have b r o u g h t them on; the
physician should have a family history. F i r s t h e
needs an accurate description o f t h e seizures. He
may then ask if any blood relatives have seizures, or
any other form of nervous disorders. H e will need

information relative to any head injuries or birth difficulties. High fevers and concussions should be noted. He may test nerve stimulation. After the preliminary phases of the examination are completed; the doctor may advise a brain wave test with the electroencephalogram.

The electroencephalogram is the most used and useful diagnostic tool in discovering epilepsy. The E.E.G. allows the physician to observe the brain and the epileptic discharge through a pattern of marks on the graph. The brain waves are transferred from the brain through electrodes (on certain areas of the brain) to the electroencephalograph where the pattern of the discharging neurons is revealed. If the E.E.G. pattern and other factors indicate a need for further examination, the physician will determine what route to follow.

Therapy for Epilepsy

After a person is diagnosed as epileptic; immediate action should be taken by the doctor to control the seizures. Epilepsy probably cannot as yet be cured, but the seizures generally can be controlled in approximately 80 percent of the cases.

Each epileptic must find the medication suitable for his case. For some it takes a short time to find the right medication, while others have many failures before an effective anticonvulsant is found. Effective drugs, though, if taken as prescribed, can control the seizures. When seizures are controlled, irregular E.E.G. patterns are still evident. The medication merely keeps the disturbance from spreading.

Nothing about epilepsy is permanent; it changes greatly. It has a tendency to clear up with increasing age, but if it does not d i s a p p e a r; it is more l i k e l y to move into the area of vulnerability most common to the specific age of the individual.

The e p i l e p t i c must be responsible for taking the medication. H i s life w i l l need to i n c l u d e regularity of meals, necessary rest, and recreational pursuits. There is indication that a busy brain and an active body reduce the number of seizures; there-fore, the individual w i t h epilepsy can operate suc-cessfully in our society w i t h a minimum of physical drawbacks.

Personality and Behavioral Aspects of Epilepsy

The epileptic is considered a n o r m a l, healthy individual u n t i l he has a seizure. Suddenly he is disabled. The nature of epilepsy i s such that he is never quite sure whether he will remain "normal," o r may suddenly, with little warning, become incapacita-ted. This is a major problem in adjustment. The epi-leptic, except f o r his seizures, is not necessarily handicapped in any w ay. H e operates in the area of normality. S o c i e t y places the epileptic into t h e a r e a of the handicapped; consequently, his position in society is often determined by this p l a c e m e n t. T h e r e f o r e, his role is a changing one, and he may never be sure whether he is healthy or ill.

There are other b e h a v i o r a l traits that a r e physiologically related t o epilepsy; post-convulsive symptoms a r e frequently confused w i t h behavior and personality disorders. Petit m a l seizures indicate a lack of concentration and daydreaming. Psychomotor seizures may result in bazaar behavior. Children in school may be referred to as l a z y, inattentive stu-dents because t h e teacher is unaware of h i s seizure

114

characteristics.

The age of onset in epileptic cases is also a factor in personality. When the symptoms begin before age three or four, personality disorders almost never appear to be primary; but they may assume an increasing importance as time goes on. The child with epilepsy may see any illness or minor physical sensation as a threat. He may perceive every ache and pain as the dread aura which preceeds the loss of consciousness. Therefore, it is felt that seizures may have a direct impact on behavior and personality.

Certainly the physical limitations placed on the epileptic alter his behavior. His activities must be limited to those that do not involve high places or any similar situations where an attack could result in serious injury. Unless his seizures are definitely controlled, the epileptic should not drive a car. The importance of driving in our society places restrictions on those who cannot operate an automobile.

Sociologically Related Factors

The first social contacts the child makes are those of the family. Here the child learns attitudes, develops a self concept, and evaluates his environment. From these attitudes and evaluations he develops a self concept. The problems of the epileptic child are made particularly difficult by lack of community resources, public indifference, and even aversion to diseases, and lack of insight on the part of the parents into the behavioral problems of their children.

The parents of a disabled child accept or reject him with varying degrees. The child will assume a role assigned him by the parents. He may be rejected more readily by the parents because they may feel guilty about some real or imagined trans-gression of morality which has resulted in their disabled child. Other parents may refuse to admit there is any disability and ignore any reference to the seizures. Finally, there are parents who do accept the child for what he is, love and care for him, and help him become a fairly secure individual.

After the parents have established an attitude toward the child, they seem to react in several different ways. Poor training is a common cause of behavior difficulties. The parents overindulge or ignore the child and assess no limits. The reaction of some parents is just the opposite. They ignore the seizures and encourage the child to compete with other less handicapped children. They push him forward in school and refuse to consider grade repetition. They hold him to standards used for an older and more intelligent child. In a normal child, these sets of circumstances would probably lead to maladjustments of various kinds. Similarly, the handicap that results from personality maladjustments in patients with epilepsy tends to grow worse as the years pass.

The family must give support and structure to this child. There should be certain helpful schedules set. The home can supply the epileptic with confidence and security, or drive him farther along the road to discontent or invalidism. Since epilepsy has a social stigma, the person is often rejected in school, or while seeking an occupation. These repeated rebuffs may lead to timidity, or to irritations and anger e n d i n g in aggressiveness and anti-social behavior. Because h i s condition i s socially stigmatized, he hides it.

Psychologically Related Factors

Not all children w i l l be affected to any great extent by e p i l e p s y. There may be a difference in reactions of children that predisposes them to severe personality development. There are certainly differences in the way each individual perceives his disability, himself, a n d the world around him; which is true with any individual.

Recurrence of seizures at unexpected a n d embarrassing times destroys confidence a n d inhibits freedom of action. N o r m a l feelings give way under the impact, he withdraws into a s h e l l of solitude, a n d limits his activities to home and the immediate neighborhood. H i s reactions to others tend to grow increasingly different.

Education

For the child with epilepsy, there are many advantages in attending s c h o o l and not being segregated as "different." If he can learn to accept his handi – cap as something to be d e a l t with and not to be resented, he has learned an important lesson in community living. The attitude of the school toward epilepsy can do much to make or break the future o f the e pi-leptic child. Current literature concerned with the education o f epileptics s h o w s a growing t r e n d in education to accept the epileptic child in the normal classroom.

Prior to the 1930's, children with seizures d i d not attend school; usually at the desire of the parents. If the child had seizures, but they did not occur during the school situation; the child attended school but knowledge of his d i s a b i l i t y was not given to school authorities. In s o m e cities, even t o d a y, epileptics are automatically excluded from the school on the recommendation of the principal and teacher.

The teacher is often the key factor in the acceptance or rejection of the epileptic in the school pro-g r a m. Although no longer consciously influenced by ancient attitudes, teachers are often averse to accepting a child with epilepsy in their classrooms. They feel he will i n t e r r u p t the class and frighten the other children. The fallacy of t h e s e attitudes lie in the realization that c h i l d r e n ' s reactions are often conditioned by the teacher. If she reacts w i t h fear or horror at the sight of a seizure this will be the reaction of the children. If the teacher accepts seizures and treats them matter-of-factly, t h e children will follow suit.

As a teacher, you should be a w a r e that a child with seizures c a n present problems in your classroom if you can't conduct yourself with understanding a n d acceptance. You must realize that a child with petit mal seizures may stare, drop his pencil, appear inattentive, etc.; all of w h i c h can interfere with h i s learning. If a child were to have a petit mal seizure of three to five seconds just as you said two t i m e s two is four, and you asked him the answer, he naturally would not know. T h e r e f o r e, don't charge a child with problem labels. He cannot a v o i d having lost those few seconds, and he may have many seizures throughout a school day, which means he has lost considerable teaching information. The child with petit mal seizures may manifest his condition with such subtleness that the teacher doesn't recognize his having seizures. The child with petit mal will not lose continance. He may be talking and suddenly stop and stare a few seconds and then continue his sentence without loss of continuity. This is not true with the child who has psychomotor seizures, because he may lose continuity and appear disoriented, dizzy, have veritgo symptoms, appear amnesic, etc.

I believe one of the most important aspects of classroom behavior is concerned with the child who has grand mal seizures. First, teachers, you can present something of a "What to do" program to your children in case of emergencies--illness, fire, tornado, earthquake, etc., but you do not have to single out the child who has seizures. He may never have one, but you and your class should be prepared.

If a grand mal seizure does happen in your classroom, proceed by making the child comfortable, move all furniture so he cannot hurt himself. A couple of children may be assigned to get a mop and bucket in case of loss of bladder control or vomiting. Do not try to insert anything into the child's mouth. You are not experienced to do that, and you may injure the child more than help. If he bites his tongue, it is better than having a teacher stick a pencil through his cheek. Don't worry about his swallowing his tongue, there is little danger involved. If he does swallow his tongue, it would probably go on down the esophagus rather than the trachea, and would not hurt him. You should, though, turn his head to the side if he accumulates fluids in the mouth. Don't try restraining his movement. When he has completed his activity he will probably be very fatigued and should have a place to lie down and rest. Most importantly, teachers, remain calm. Do not panic your children or yourself, and use some common sense judgement. Children will accept and work with you in these emergencies if you have created an awareness of what to expect.

After he completes his public schooling, the epileptic child may decide to apply for acceptance to a college or university. Again, he may face difficulties; not because of ability, but because he puts on his application blank the condemning word, "epilepsy." As a whole, schools of higher education differ in acceptance of epileptics. There are several factors which influence the acceptance or rejection of the epileptic into the program of the college. The type of education offered, size of student body, section of the country, presence or absence of a department of student health, and previous experience with epileptics determine the policies. Colleges who accept epileptics most readily, are liberal arts colleges with large student bodies.

In summary, it is safe to say that the major change which must come about is in the public evaluation of epilepsy. It is up to parents, teachers, counselors, doctors, and epileptic individuals themselves, to know what epilepsy is and to help create a more accurate picture of epilepsy to the general public.

EXHIBITIONISM

Quite often the first response an individual experiences when a sexual offender is sought or captured is one of disgust and anger toward the person who is breaking our social codes. An exhibitionist is one of these social deviates. This deviation constitutes the largest group of those apprehended by the police for sexual offenses each year.

In exhibitionism, sexual pleasure is achieved through exposure of the genitals in public or semipublic places, usually to members of the opposite sex or to children. Sometimes the demonstrations are accompanied by suggestive gestures or masturbatory activity, but more commonly there is only exposure.

The exposure may take place in some secluded location like a park or in a more public place, such as a department store, church, theater, or bus. In cities the exhibitionist may drive his car by schools or bus stops, exhibit hinself while in the car, and then drive rapidly away. In many cases the exposure is made under fairly constant conditions, such as only in churches or buses, or in the same general vicinity and at the same time of day. The sex object, too, is usually fairly consistent--ordinarily a stranger of the opposite sex, falling within a particular age range.

Exhibitionism appears to be most common during the warm spring and summer months and occurs primarily among young adult males. Practically all occupational groups are represented, including engineers, teachers, students, salesmen, mechanics, and unskilled laborers. A m o n g women exhibitionism of the genitals is relatively r a r e, and those cases that do o c c u r are less likely to be reported to the police than are offenses made by male exhibitionists. Of course, many of the young males are not immediately reported, and sometimes they are even encouraged by their victims. Usually, however, the offender is reported. Even though exhibitionists constitute the largest group apprehended f o r sexual offenses, t h e actual dynamics involved are far from clear.

The following etiological a s p e c t s of exhibitionism offered by Coleman, (1964), may be n o t e d and examined for cause:

1. M a n y preadolescent boys who engage in s e x play, either of a homosexual or heterosexual nature, begin with the exhibition of the genitalia.

2. Most exhibitionists s e e m to feel strongly that masturbation is sinful and evil and d o not usually experience any p l e a s u r e from masturbation unless it is p e r f o r m e d as a part of genital exhibition.

3. The individual o f t e n struggles against the impulse to expose himself in m u c h the same way that the adolescent struggles a g a i n s t the impulse to masturbate, b u t as the s e x- ual tension rises, he feels c o m p e l l e d to carry out h i s exhibitionistic activities. And as in the case of masturbation, he often feels guilty and remorseful afterwards, particularly i f h e has achieved ejaculation.

4. T h e suspense, excitement, a n d apprehension surrounding t h e exhibition of t h e genitals

often intensify or reinforce its sexually stimulating aspects. In this connection it is interesting to note that indecent exposure is the only type of sexual crime which increases when the papers are playing up a "sex crime wave."

5. Signs of being impressed or of emotional shock on the part of the victim are eagerly looked for by the exhibitionists. When his activities are ignored he is usually disappointed and abashed. But, since many women react with disgust and obvious emotional shock, the exhibitionist is not usually disappointed.

6. The typical exhibitionist is apparently a quiet, submissive, "nice" individual with strong feelings of inadequacy, inferiority, and insecurity in personal relations. He usually comes from a strict home environment, has adopted puritanical attitudes toward sex, and is often overly attached to a domineering mother.

7. Although statistics indicate that approximately one-half of the exhibitionists are married, they usually fail to achieve satisfactory sexual relations with their wives. Many state that they married only because of family pressure; many have married at a relatively late age.

There are apparently three major dynamic factors underlying exhibitionism. First, in many cases the exhibitionism seems to represent an immature approach to the opposite sex based upon inadequate information, puritanical attitudes toward masturbation and sexual relations, marked feelings of shyness and inferiority, and often overattachment to the mother.

Coleman (1964) cites the following example of exhibitionism:

A highschool teacher had exhibited himself for several months to a 30-year-old woman who lived next door. She finally reported him, and before arresting him, the police took motion pictures of his activities from the woman's apartment. In order to get clearer picturers they raised the window. At this point the teacher thought he had finally made an impression and in turn raised his own window and intensified his masturbatory activities and suggestive gestures.

After his arrest he revealed a background of overattachment to a domineering mother and an inhibited, puritanical attitude toward sex. He had rarely gone out with girls and felt extremely shy and insecure in his approach to them. His strong bond to his mother undoubtedly contributed to his difficulties in heterosexual adjustment, making even his fantasies of sexual relations with other women seem like acts of unfaithfulness toward his mother. Yet his strong attitudes against masturbation gave him no adequate outlet for the discharge of his sexual tensions. As a result, he apparently blundered into his awkward, immature, and socially unacceptable form of sexual behavior.

Closely related to this background of immaturity and overattachment to the mother is the second major dynamic factor, doubts and fears about one's masculinity. As a result of his strong female identification, together with the common fears and scruples about masturbatory activities, the exhibitionist has a strong need to demonstrate his masculinity and potency.

Alpfelberg (1944) cited the case of a patient who received sexual satisfaction only when he accompanied the exhibition of his genitals with a question to his victim as to whether she had ever seen such a large penis. On one occasion the woman, instead of evidencing shock and embarrassment looked at him scornfully and assured him that she had. On this occasion the defendant stated that he received no sexual gratification. Such common experiences as "Making her sit up and take notice" bear witness to the importance to these individuals of proving their "masculinity" and "potency."

Besides expressing immaturity or doubts about masculinity or both, exhibitionism may be only a part of more serious psychopathology. For example, Henniger (1941) in an analysis of 51 cases of indecent exposure found eight of them psychotic, ten of them mentally retarded, four chronically alcholic, and three psychopathic. The remaining 19, he classified as emotionally immature. It would appear that conditions which lower restraints, weaken the individuals repressive forces or lead to personality regression, which may eventuate in open exhibitionistic activities in predisposed personalities.

In very occasional cases another factor, hostility is considered. The exhibitionistic activity appears to afford an outlet for hostile impulses toward members of the opposite sex or toward society in general. Instead of fire-setting, stealing, or other antisocial acts, the individual exhibits himself as a retaliation against rejections and frustrations which he attributes to others. In such cases, the exhibitionism may be accompanied by aggressive acts, and the victim may be knocked down or otherwise attacked, but this behavior is rare. Ordinarily, the behavior is limited to exposure, so that exhibitionists are not usually the dangerous psychopaths that many newspaper stories make them out to be. Typically, he's a quiet, submissive, "nice" individual who feels inadequate in personal and sexual relationships, (Coleman, 1960).

These arrests usually bring the community to arms in order to punish the "captured sex fiend." In reality, most of these cases are men who because of age or other reasons, are lacking sexual potency and are not likely to hurt anyone physically. However, a severe psychological shock may be given a child who encounters an exhibitionist, (Strange, 1965).

Some psychoanalysts believe exhibitionism to be the result of castration anxiety that is so great that the person constantly needs to reassure himself that he still has his sexual organ (or power) by exposing it and experiencing the traumatic reactions of others. The exhibitionist thus gains not only the sexual pleasure through the exhibitionistic act, but also punishes other people (causes them anxiety) to make them atone for his own anxieties.

During puberty and early adolescence, and even in earlier periods, (especially the phallic period), exhibitionistic acts among children are commonplace,

but childhood curiosity doesn't have the same significance that exhibitionism does when it occurs in an
adult (Hutt and Gibby, 1957). During the early form-
ative period all normal children are curious about
their bodies and will examine the bodies of other
children. If parents look upon these exploratory
interests for what they are--finding out about one's
self and one's world--and treat the behavior in the
same way they treat evidences of the child's growing
interests, no special problem will be likely to develop in this regard, (Hutt and Gibby, 1959).

In a study by Mohr, reported by Rosen (1965) on
exhibitionists treated at an out-patient clinic, the
age distribution showed two peaks; one peak in adolescence and the other in the twenties. The adolescent patients were unmarried, but nearly all the young
adults had married prior to the onset of exhibitionism. The major precipitants of exhibitionism in the
latter group were impending or had recent birth of a
child, unsatisfactory sexual relations, or the threat
of sexual deprivation attendant on the birth of their
child. Mohr's data are consistent with the impres −
sion of many investigators that the urge to exposure
occurs when the individual is in conflict with a female, a domineering mother in adolescence, and the
wife or future wife in the twenties. It has been
noted by investigators that the wife of the exhibitionist frequently is a mother substitute who dom-
inates her self-effacing unaggressive husband.

Punishment for these "crimes" does not have
positive effects, but punishment may do considerable
damage to the individual. The most effective way of
remediation is through psychotherapy. With this

knowledge available, and the facilities a v a i l a b l e throughout the United States, it is a s e r i o u s mistake when t h e s e individuals do not receive the help that they need and w a n t , and most of them do w a n t help. Therefore, through t h e education of the public, more of these individuals c o u l d be reached and helped by providing better pre-natal and early childhood education programs for families.

REFERENCES

Apfelberg, B., Sugar C. and Pfeffer, A.A., "A Psychiatric Study of 250 Sex Offenders," American Journal of Psychiatry, vo. 100, 1944.

Coleman, James C. Abnormal Psychology and Modern Life, Chicago: Scott-Foresman and Co., 3rd edition, 1964.

_____, Personality Dynamics and Effective Behavior, Chicago: Scott-Foresman and Co., 1960.

Henniger, J.M., "Exhibitionism," Journal of Criminal Psychopathology, vol. 2, 1941.

Hutt, Max L. and Gibby, Gwyn, R., Patterns of Abnormal Behavior, Boston: Allyn and Bacon, Inc., 1957.

_____, The Child, Development and Adjustment, Boston: Allyn and Bacon, Inc., 1959.

Rosen, Ephraim and Gregory, Ian, Abnormal Psychology. Philadelphia: W. B. Saunders Co., 1965.

Strange, Jack Roy, Abnormal Psychology, Understanding Behavior Disorders, New York: McGraw-Hill Book Co., 1965.

FETISHISM

The word fetish was originally applied to inanimate objects worshipped by primitive people which were believed by them to possess magical qualities. From this approach the definition was extended to include the shorter Oxford English Dictionary, to mean, "Something irrationally reverenced."

A person in love may be said to treat his beloved as if she had magical qualities and to revere her irrationally; but he is not on this account a fetishist. The term fetishism is applied to a sexual deviation in which magic appears to reside, not in the entire person, but in a part of the person, an object connected with the person, or a symbolic substitute for the person. The fetishist may feel a compulsive and irrational sexual attraction toward an inanimate object, such as a glove or shoe; or he may be fascinated by some part of the body, other than the genitals, such as the hair or breast. In some instances deformity or damage to the body may be a focus of attraction, as in the case in which a man was erotically aroused by boys who were crippled and had to wear leg irons. More rarely, a particular action performed by a person may become a sexual stimulus which is e q u i v a l e n t to a fetish; and cases have been r e p o r t e d in which smoking o r coughing has been associated with sexual arousal.

Fetishism i s a deviation which is g e n e r a l l y confined to the male s e x.   I t is only a t r u e de- v i a t i o n when the fetish itself is totally substi- tuted for a person. Most fetishists are heterosexual but homosexual fetishism also exists. There are many different things that male homosexuals m a y establish as a fetish.   For many homosexual males, t h e penis itself becomes a fetish.   Minor degrees of fetishism can be detected in many men, and there p r o b a b 1 y is no point at which one can say that n o r m a 1 i t y ends and p a t h o 1 o g y begins.   Any special feature o f a woman upon which a man's erotic attention i s focused may in a sense, be called a fetish.   A fetish may be an undergarment, a p i e c e of jewelry, a p a r t i c u l a r kind of m a t e r i a 1, or a part of the body.   In each case it is e i t h e r a substitution of a p a r t for a whole; therefore, the fetish a t t r a c t s the emotion which would normally be directed t o w a r d a complete person; or else it a r o u s e s the same feelings which in the ordinary man are evoked by the female genitals.

In "normal" people, the garments or parts of the b o d y, which to the d e v i a n t are likely to be come fetishes, serve to attract attention and to a r o u s e interest.   If this interest is reciprocated, it m a y soon e x t e n d to include the whole person with par- ticular emphasis upon the g e n i t a l s . For the fet- i s h i s t this extension of interest is p r o b a b l y blocked; consequently, his interest s t o p s short at, and becomes f o c u s e d upon the fetish.   The fetish, then, to him significantly pertains t o the person as a whole or to one's genitals.   Therefore, instead of his erotic interest spreading, it remains obsessively fixed upon the fetish or the part of the person which happens to appeal to him.

Generally it has been established that the fetish has its origin in very early childhood; and considerable attention h a s been given to this theory by pre-Freudian writers, who c o n c e i v e d of fetishism as a kind of conditioned r e f l e x. Thus, if a child had accidentally been erotically aroused by the f e e l of his mother's s i l k dress, by the s i g h t of his sister's underclothes, or by the t o u c h or smell of the rubber sheet w h i c h lay beneath him in his cot; it was supposed that he might forever remain sensitized to one of these particular objects, and would therefore demand its presence, (Starr, 1964).

T h e fact that fetishism is almost entirely confined to the male m a y also be related to the process of conditioning. The human male seems to be sexually responsive to a w i d e r range of stimuli than the female, and seems also to be more e a s i l y conditioned by t h e s e stimuli. In g e n e r a l, women tend to be indifferent to sexual stimuli which do not i n c l u d e e i t h e r physical caresses or an element of romance. They may enjoy reading sentimental novels and respond to films. They may become e x c i t e d by pornography, by e r o t i c pictures, by nudity or physical display, or by a variety of other sexual stimuli which appeal to the visual sense and to the e r o t i c imagination.

The psychoanalytic explanation o f fetishism i s in terms of the castration complex--a basic aboriginal fear which can be detected in every one of us; but which, supposedly, is particularly emphasized in the fetishist. The c a s t r a t i o n complex is one of the cornerstones of psychoanalysis. Freud explained the fetishist as being so especially terrified of castration that he was compelled to pretend to himself that women r e a l l y had penises in spite of his knowledge that t h e y did not; and that the fetish a c t e d as a reassurance by representing the missing female penis, (Rose, 1964).

Women have no need for f e t i s h e s because they do n o t have to achieve or sustain an erection. The fears from which they s u f f e r and which may impair their s e x u a l enjoyment and performance are equally important, but they do not include this s p e c i f i c difficulty; and it is probably t h i s fact, combined with the greater responsiveness o f men to v i s u a l and other sexual stimuli, which accounts for the male monopoly of fetishism, (Rosen, 1964).

M a n y fetishes have a sadomasochistic significance, (Karpman, 1962). T h e history o f feminine fashion is full of devices which n o t only accentuate f e m a l e sexual characteristics, but a l s o restrict movement to the point of discomfort. The high-heeled shoe, which is probably the most common fetish of all, is one example of this. Impractical, uncomfortable, highly restrictive, it s h o r t e n s the stride, makes walking any distance impossible, and n e e d s frequent repair. Nevertheless, high heels are such a potent weapon in the feminine armory o f devices t o attract men, even t h e structure of airplanes, and the floors of buildings h a v e to be modified so that women c a n w e a r them without doing too much damage. Many feminine fashions are designed to make women appear more fragile and helpless than they actually are; and this appeals to men because it puts them in t h e superior position--one in which they can be protective, dominant, and physically more active.

All degrees of fetishism exist, from the true deviation, in which the fetish is substituted for the person and simply used for masturbation, to the much more common condition in which the fetish serves simply as a means by which the man can be sure that his desire will be fully aroused and that he will be potent enough to fulfill it. There are many men with mild degrees of fetishism who, during intercourse, have recourse to fantasies in which the fetish plays some part. This is especially so when they are fatigued, or when, for some reason, intercourse is not proving wholly satisfactory. Since those who suffer from fetishistic compulsions usually have an abnormal degree of sexual guilt; it is often difficult for them to admit their particular preferences to their partners; or if they can bring themselves to do so they do it in such a way that the female also regards the request for her to wear a particular scent or a particular garment as abnormal, (Karpman, 1962).

Fetishism has a compulsive quality; and, indeed, the phantasy which accompanies the fetish may be compared with an obsessional thought. Like the latter, it is not deliberately willed, it is often alien to the person's conscious intention, and the man who suffers from it frequently wants to be rid of it. Many fetishists show other features of the obsessional character; rigidity, meticulousness, a fear of dirt, and a tendency to hoard. Naturally enough, one of the things which may be hoarded is the fetish; and there are cases reported of people who make enormous collections of shoes, pigtails, or other fetish objects. The connection between this and normal "collecting" is interesting, and analysis might reveal that many collections of stamps, matchboxes, wine labels, and other objects which are not commonly fetishes, have a sexual significance at an unconscious level, (Karpman, 1962).

Occasionally, the desire for the fetish provokes stealing and some of the more bizarre thefts, such as those of women's underclothes from washing lines are the work of fetishists pursuing their aberrations. In general, however, fetishists are timid people who live withdrawn lives and do not harm anyone; and since every man harbors within himself a form of fetishism, it is hoped that a greater understanding may cause a compassioned response to this sexual deviation.

REFERENCES

Karpman, Benjamin, M. D. The Sexual Offender and His Offenses, Julian Press, Inc., 1962.

Rosen, Ismond, M. D., D. P. M., Sexual Deviation, The Pathology and Treatment of, 1964, Oxford University Press.

Starr, Anthony, Sexual Deviation, Copyright, 1964, Cox and Wyman, LTD., London, Fakenham and Reading.

HOMOSEXUALITY

Bryan Magee, (1966) defines homosexuality as: ". . .a condition of the personality, not of the body. It consists in an abnormal development such that the individual is sexually aroused by, and prone to become emotionally fixated on (i.e. fall in love with) members of his or her own sex. . ." He goes on to state: ". . .people who have sexual relations with partners of either sex are known as bisexual. These are considerably fewer than one might expect. The great majority of homosexuals are exclusively homosexual." Many authorities feel that people who are bisexual in adult life must be people whose original bias was also toward homosexuality.

Quite a large proportion of the human race does regard bisexuality as a norm. It is definitely taboo in the Christian countries, but these account for only a minority of people. The Muslim countries for instance, s e e m to accept bisexuality as common-place. It is common knowledge that the Ancient Greek were bisexual.

Magee (1966) also feels that a handful of cases being homosexual does not represent a decision. He feels one does not choose to be or not to be a homo-sexual. An e x a m p l e of his opinion is cited among people of the same sex being c o n f i n e d together in prison, the armed forces, boarding schools, and other such institutions. The homosexuality in some public schools is of the same kind. What is in evidence in these cases is not homosexuality, but simply sexuality. The people concerned have n o r m a l sexual drives, a normal need to give expression of these p h y s i c a l needs, but they are in an environment in which the only people they c a n have sexual relations with are members of their own sex.

Young boys get crushes on older or younger boys, and hero worship sportsmen, athletes, or other public figures. These problems are probably manifested most often in gym classes. Teachers should be aware of these signs and work c l o s e l y with students who show over attention to these areas and people. This stage of development probably contains an important element of narcissism. At this stage the child is fascinated not only by his own feelings, but by his own body, by his developing genitalia, and discoveries of feel-ings. The homosexual stage through which people pass is normal--it is not the same thing as being homosex-ual. H o w e v e r, it should somewhat help the rest of us--teachers, doctors, parents, etc.--to understand what being a homosexual is like.

Some observations indicate that approximately

one man in three has had a homosexual experience at least once in his life--usually in adolescence, but occassionally later. A slightly less frequent incidence, but still a somewhat large proportion of women, indicate homosexual experiences. "Science News" (1969) states four possible definitions of homosexuality.

1. At the beginning of the century it was thought that the problem was of constitutional nature, because of the fact that glands from the opposite sex had been implanted in animals with sexual deviations indicated that a possible glandular imbalance in humans could account for certain humans having sexual desires for a member of the same sex.

2. Franz Kollman (1952) ran an experiment with homosexual twins. He found that those born from the same zygote were significantly more similar in pattern than were fraternal twins. From this experiment scientists concluded that a physical predisposition is there. How society reacts then determines the extent to which humans desire sexual relations with members of the same sex.

3. Research done by Dr. Irving Bieber from 1952 -1957 supports the theory set forth by Freud. Freud believed that families in which the mother is seductive, but antisexual, and makes her son a confidant and shows preference to him over her husband, is thereby crushing his independence. This puts the son in a position of being ignored by his father because of the competition for the

mother's attention. Such a problem may bring about a situation which encourages a latent homosexual to run from normal development and become a person who desires relations only with members of the same sex. The psychoanalytic view has always indicated that male homosexuality is predominantly because of hidden but incapacitating fears of the opposite sex. Freud felt the causes of homosexuality would have to be sought in early childhood.

4. Evelyn Hooker of UCLA states that fear of the opposite sex, fear of responsibility, and flight from reality, and destructiveness cause a person to focus his attentions on members of the opposite sex.

Even though no common cause can be focused upon by all authorities it seems the definition is universal. A homosexual is a person, male or female, who desires sexual gratification from members of the same sex.

For many years homosexuality has been looked upon as a crime and a problem to be greatly feared. One concept was that all homosexuals were effeminate in character with high pitched voices, and could be easily spotted in a crowd of people. Except for the fact that homosexuality is generally considered a crime, punishable by imprisonment for periods ranging from a few days to life, most of these stereotyped concepts are false. Today the awareness is becoming more pronounced that trying to cure a homosexual by placing him in prison is like trying to cure an alcoholic by locking him in a distillery.

138

Only in a few instances do homosexuals have an interest in small children. They are usually very careful in attempting to contact other homosexuals. The partners that homosexuals seem to prefer are similar in age range to the choice of heterosexuals. A large number may go through a period in adolescence or early manhood when they prefer relations with older people. Usually during most of their adult lives they prefer partners of the same age range; and then to an increasing extent as the years go by they are sexually attracted to younger partners.

Contrary to popular belief, homosexuals cannot be easily spotted in crowds. Male homosexuals for example often are just as masculine in appearance as any other male in a crowd. They do not limit them- selves to particular types of work--the homosexual can be found in every walk of life.

As homosexuals proceed into their thirties and forties, they often become increasingly lonely and upset. At this time they find it more difficult to form stable affectionate relationships with other homosexuals. During this period they may marry and cease their overt homosexual activities. Others continue their homosexual activities throughout their married life. Superficially they may function fairly well as husbands and fathers, and wives and mothers.

Some social advantages are considered if one is homosexual. For example, he can have a much higher standard of living, because each member of the part- nership has his own income. Rent and bills are usu- ally shared. If a man is dating a girl, theater tick- ets, dinner checks, and all the expected niceties are very expensive. All these expenses are shared if the partners of the same sex are living together.

The loneliness that is sometimes felt by single heterosexual people does not have to be felt by homosexuals. Upon entering any city or country, just slight inquiry will lead them to gay bars or contact with other homosexuals. Crossing lines of social class makes no difference to homosexuals. They are a minority and therefore, are anxious to meet other members of the social minority whether of the same social class or not.

The biggest disadvantage of being a homosexual is the fear of being discovered. One serious result of being a homosexual is that they are open to blackmail. This effect engenders guilt and self-contempt in many cases. It also adds an element of defiance-- mainly defiance of society. Married people who carry on homosexual activities have greater fears. Their fears do not stem from the fact that they feel what they are doing is wrong, but they fear the fact that if they are caught the possibilities of public knowledge and/or prosecution could bring humiliation to their families. There is also the constant fear of losing their jobs and respectable positions in their community, which in many cases can never be regained wherever they may go.

Society generally has the idea that homosexuals are strictly out for the sexual act only, which isn't true. Homosexuals have similar emotional and sensual feelings as heterosexual partners. The difference, of course, is that they have these feelings for the same sex. Many people indicate that it is impossible for them to visualize members of the same sex making love to each other. This may be true, but likewise, when we were children and learned that the stork did not b r i n g us, but we were the result of a sexual act between our parents, we probably suffered difficulty visualizing our parents performing the sex act.

As heterosexuals do, homosexuals also seek companionship, security, acceptance, etc., other than just the sex act itself. Homosexuals, in performing the act of sexual intercourse, spend the greater proportion of the time cuddling, kissing, fondling, and caressing. Kinsey's s t u d i e s indicated that orgasm many times was not achieved, nor totally enjoyed by a large number of homosexuals.

M o s t homosexual couples have the same type of household arrangement as heterosexual couples. One partner takes on the m a s c u l i n e, aggressive role of making the d e c i s i o n s for the couple. Often, this becomes so significant that one partner almost assumes the role of a child. The relationship of which party is aggressive and which is passive may occur because of age; however, it appears more often when a large gap exists between social class and education. It is not unusual for one or the other to have a strong dislike for either penis insertion or acceptance; whichever the case may be, one will assume the other role. Some male homosexuals will assume either passive, o r aggressive roles.

N a t u r a l l y, much more fear and anxiety is felt by homosexual couples t h a n by heterosexual couples. Their fears of discovery and blackmail cause them to avoid fusses or clashes with such people as landlords, neighbors, or anything else which m a y d r a w attention to themselves. For these reasons, they must be prepared to put up with much more disturbance than the heterosexuals would. However, it does appear as the younger generation changes, that there is a trend toward somewhat more acceptance and understanding of this minority group in our society.

Most of these people do not form lasting relationships. Jealousy is prominent among heterosexuals, which in the end usually destroys the partnership. There is no binding ceremony in the presence of a congregation that society deems binding forever, so no legal action is necessary to end the relationship. Therefore, infidelity of one or both of the partners seems prominent.

It has been found that most homosexuals have guilt feelings of one sort or another. This is not unusual, because we are conditioned from an early age to regard homosexuality as something sinful, or wrong, or at least freakish. People find it hard to live in a society which stigmatizes something one does as both filthy and immoral. Almost all homosexuals know that their parents would be horrified if they knew of their activity. This knowledge alone is enough, expecially in adolescence, to create serious feelings of guilt.

The homosexual population is more prone than the general population to psychiatric disorders such as anxiety states, psychosomatic illness, depressions, schizophrenic reactions, and other major psychiatric problems. Homosexuals are often unable to accept the responsibilities of life. They are often carefree and happy-go-lucky until a crisis arises. At such times they must have someone to make their decisions. They are often petty and easily angered by their partners. Because of these characteristics, they are often compared to children who live for their wants and desires alone. Depression about themselves and long spells of self-pity are not uncommon. Often they are prone to lead an almost manic-depressive life. Homosexuals in many instances are self-centered, self-indulgent, and many times almost totally unaware of other people's desires or wishes. They find it very difficult to stand on their own, outside their own tribe. The homosexuals have underlying hostility to persons of both sexes, and even toward their own partners. This clearly shows why some homosexual attachments tend to be unstable.

Homosexuals are rarely motivated to change their behavior. They want to keep their homosexuality in much the same sense that heterosexuals want to keep their heterosexual capacities. Psychiatric treatment rarely changes their homosexual status. Even when motivated to seek help they will usually remain homosexual, but can often be helped with some overlying emotional problems--such as reaching a more comfortable adjustment within the framework of their deviation. A therapist obviously can do little to ameliorate the basic personality distortion. However, he can sometimes give them help for their depressions, psychosomatic symptoms, or obsessive disorders. Often they can be helped with their emotional problems without any attempt to change their homosexuality.

The homosexual in Western society has, like other minorities, always lived as an outsider. He is often denied civil rights, driven from small towns, and fired from valuable jobs. In short, if a person is a homosexual, that characteristic is likely to be the most powerful and influential factor in his life; more than the condition of wealth, poverty, or intelligence.

Society can no longer hide from the d e f i n i t e fact that homosexuality exists. The fact seems apparent that they have produced a culture that, to say the lease, is curious in its characteristics and aims. This culture has had an i n f l u e n c e upon the dress, art, and literature of the middle class society.

The following general description somewhat seems to summarize the dilemma of one's being a homosexual: Homosexuals, in a bizarre psychological turnabout have seemingly achieved a life style that integrates and proves the dictum, "You become what you are." W i t h a culture which appears to be based on nothing m o r e than a brutal caricature of the femaleness he so violently rejects; the absolute craziness of it all, is that he sometimes, has become the woman he despises. Thus he has won by losing.

Ask yourself, teachers and parents, as a heterosexual, if I were to go into a therapist's office and ask him to change me into a homosexual, w o u l d that be possible? M a k e the same analogy with the homosexual wh o goes into therapy to change into a heterosexual. It is apparent that the task would be tremendous. O n e more question, if you have a homosexual student in your classroom: how will you react?

REFERENCES

Magee, Bryan. One In Twenty - A study of Homosexuality in Men and Women. Stein and Day, New York, 1966.

Massett, L., "Homosexuality Changes on the Way," Science News, December 13, 1969.

Shoemaker, "Operation to Relieve Perversion," Science News, January 10, 1970.

Reuben, David. Everything You Always Wanted to Know About Sex, Reiss Publications: New York, 1969.

Teachers need to learn more about disorders that affect the total development of children. We may sometimes tend to overlook important factors which very directly alter the social development and learning in our schools. Everyone in the educational profession must cooperate and become more open-minded concerning the total development of our children.

Educators agree that since the whole child goes to school, the school should have as its aims the development of children to their fullest capacities. To fulfill this objective, the elementary schools should become more aware of all psychiatric disorders. There are in the United States today, thousands of men, women, and children who are worrying habitually over ailments they have never had, and will probably die of something that they have never feared. Most of them prescribe for themselves. They generally have a well-stocked medicine cabinet, the daily irrigation, the tonic, or the laxative. They provide the chief support of the patent-medicine industry which, with its advertising media, can boast of annual receipts running into the millions.

Contrary to popular belief, body overconcern is by no means confined to the idle and the well-to-do. It drains also the pocketbooks of individuals and families in the moderate and low income groups. Far more serious, though, than the financial waste, is the reduced social effectiveness which inevitably results when a person is perpetually concerned about his own health.

Hypochondriacal disorders are characterized by habitual preoccupation with a supposed disease or defect in an organ or body part which is actually functioning within normal limits, or by habitually exaggerated concern over organs or body parts which are defective or diseased. The varieties of body overconcern are endless. Almost any organ, system, part, or function may be unjustifiably accused by the patient--the gastrointestinal system and its associated glands, the heart and blood vessels, the respiratory system, the head, the neck and back, the nervous system, the arms and hands, and the legs and feet.

As a rule a person will complain about several organs or functions. For example, the following symptoms were presented by a fourth grade girl: overly concerned with aches and pains, constantly complained of headaches and stomach cramps, complained of her eyes burning, complained of chest pains, and when the time came to exert physically some energy, she always felt sick. This behavior naturally irritated the other students in the classroom. She didn't have any close friendships. Children seldom choose other children with this disorder as their friends. When a child habitually complains and brings notes from home to excuse her from all activity she just isn't a popular child among her peers. Students have a tendency to choose other children who can participate in all school activities. Simple exercises within the classroom were too strenuous for her. Her parents obviously hadn't consulted medical help. They kept her out of school for weeks at a time for just a slight cold. After she returned to school and was asked if she had been to a doctor, she replied that she had not. She wasn't a physically sick child in appearance, but she certainly had all the complaints of an extremely ill person.

The following symptoms were presented by a 38 year old married woman. She complained of headaches, frequent and severe; aches in her limbs, backaches, poor vision, floating specks before her eyes, sinus trouble, and intermittent ringing and crackling in her ears, poor sleep, palpatations, and heart pain. She believed that her blood was not circulating freely because her arms and legs seemed to go to sleep too easily. She reported a large appetite, but poor digestion.

This person's work record is typical of a great many hypochondriacal cases. She gave up at school at the age of 13, without objection, to help her mother around the house. At 17, she was prevailed upon to take a job in a factory, but here she suffered from headaches, backaches, and pains in the chest and abdomen for which no basis in organic pathology could be found. She later married and disliked sex relations but was satisfied with routine housework. She had many acquaintances but no hobbies or interests.

Another example is a ten year old boy. He, like the girl previously mentioned, never participated with other children. He usually came to school for only half of the school day. His parents were middle-aged when he was born. He was an only child. Both his parents worked outside the home and seemed to have little time for him. He complained continuously about his head, his legs, etc. He also missed many days of school. When homework was assigned, he never had any of it completed because he was sick, which always was his excuse. He sometimes seemed to be improving if he received a lot of affection and attention. With his parents both working, maybe they just didn't have enough time for him. His complaining may simply have been a way of saying, "Pay some attention to me." Nevertheless, he certainly had many symptoms of a person afflicted with hypochondriasis.

Adults underestimate immensely the capacity of children to understand what adults say to them. Children are very sensitive to the feelings and the attitudes of persons toward them. In many ways they are more sensitive to such feelings than are adults. The physician, parent, and teacher should always assume that children have the capacity to understand nearly all that is told to them. The language one uses with children should be simple, direct, and graphic. Gestures and emphatic expressions are good. Enthusiastic interest is good. Children like someone who talks with them earnestly, jovially, and honestly. Strong reassurances and simple explanations are always indicated when dealing with children.

The person suffering with hypochondria is abnormally preoccupied with his health. He wakes up in the morning feeling exhausted. He runs from one doctor to another without benefit. His medicine cabinet is usually full of patent medicines. He is a person who enjoys his ill health. He may bitterly resent anyone telling him that he looks well. The hypochondriac's imagined illness serves as an escape mechanism to relieve him of anxieties which result from personal frustrations. Hypochondriacs whose lives have been reorganized and whose personal problems have been solved, are known to have improved miraculously so far as their health is concerned.

Discuss the child's difficulties with him through understanding and empathy. Let the child realize you know he is suffering, and then simply try to find an alternative which will replace the hypochondriacal syndrome. The child may have an extreme dislike for school; therefore, an illness gives him a defense mechanism so he won't have to do his school work. If the child knows that you know school is a bad scene for him, and that you will try to help him and make school more pleasant; he quite likely will escape many of his physically protecting complaints.

INCEST

The purpose of this dialogue is to examine the nature of the reasons for, and the results of incestuous relationships. Incestuous relationships are usually defined as culturally prohibited sexual relations between certain family members, such as brother and sister or father and daughter.

It is somewhat important to remember that a social deviation today may not have been considered as such in the past. There have been cultures in history that have not only allowed this type of social behavior, but have encouraged and in some instances,

149

required it. The scriptures and mythology texts have many examples of incestuous behavior. There are numerous acts of incest in the Old Testement. Some of these were acknowledged as sinful and punished, and some were rewarded. The children of Adam and Eve were obligated to commit incest to perpetuate the species; therefore, in theory, we have all decended from incestuous relationships.

In Greek and Roman mythology there are many examples of incest, which were usually attributed to the Gods. One of the most famous stories is that of Oedipus. The story related that Oedipus was separated in infancy from his mother, Jocasta. Later the two unknowingly married, and conceived two sons and two daughters. Then the incest became known to them and as a result Oedipus blinded himself; Jocasta committed suicide by hanging; the two sons killed each other; and the two daughters were buried alive. From this story, of course, comes the present day term, Oedipus Complex, which is commonly used by Freudian psychologists. The Oedipus Complex refers to the desire of a mother for her son, or the desire of a father for his daughter.

For thousands of years, the Egyptians engaged in incest without any obvious damage. The Egyptian royalty especially participated in brother-sister marriages. The Persians, in one period in history, had no prohibitions against incest. The old Hebrews seem to have had a tolerance for incest at one time, but gradually their enforcements were tightened. This seems also to be true of the Greeks who were once very permissive, but as time passed they became very strict in their prohibitions concerning incest. The Romans always prohibited incest, but their laws were slack at times, and were also ignored by the Nobility.

In the Middle Ages with the growing strength of Christianity, the prohibitions of incest were extended to unreasonable lengths. In Europe even sixth cousins were forbidden to marry. The result of this rule was that there were very few people in small villages who were allowed to marry, which caused more incest, especially between mothers and sons. It is also possible that since sons were needed to work at home; incest was a way a mother might encourage her son to stay in the home.

By these examples, we can plainly see the great variation of prohibitions and popular thought concerning incest during different periods in history. The greatest possible reason for these variations or inconsistencies seems to be that no one can adequately explain why or to what extent incest should be considered a crime. The arguments that it is an unnatural act or that it is biologically damaging can be debated. It appears, though, that the most significant result of incest is that it breaks down the relationships in a family unit.

It is impossible to determine the incidence of actual incest. Many cases go unreported because people within the family do not want others to know. This is especially true of those who are taking part in the relationship. Also, many cases do not become statistics, because incest is rarely prosecuted. The laws of each state are different concerning incest, and difficult at times to enforce. Some state laws imply that father-daughter incest is more serious than the other types of incest. Probably the reason for this perspective is the higher incidence of father-daughter incest in the United States. The actual incidence is a matter of estimation based on known cases and / or prosecution; but those of us who have worked with family problems realize that incest in the general population of the United States is actually quite a problem.

The concern for controlling criminal incest does not appear to be so vital when the act is between two consenting adults. The real concern is to control those cases that involve the abuse of a child. How does sexual abuse such as incest affect a developing child? How does it affect his personality, his school work, or his adult life? Behavioral studies tend to show that all types of sexual offenses against children affect them greatly. Many of these children are able to participate in sexual activities for extended periods of time (3-6 years), but they later have strong feelings of guilt. This guilt is sometimes expressed indirectly as nightmares, phobias, and general anxiety symptoms.

Incestuous father-daughter relationships may begin at early child ages varying from four to fourteen years. Most girls involved in the sexual relationships over extended periods of time fail to report the situation, and the mothers of these children also fail or are afraid to protect their daughters. Most cases come to the attention of the authorities through some external factors such as a neighbor reporting neglect of children.

Observation and clinical investigation indicates that father-daughter incest causes extreme guilt and depression. Other findings indicate that many girls have learning difficulties, some become extremely bossy, some have somatic complaints s u c h as loss of appetite and abdominal distress; and others may become sexually promiscuous. They also i n d i c a t e a confused sexual identification, and a fear of sexuality. Their main defense mechanisms are usually denial, repression, and projection.

I have worked with a number of teenagers who have been sexually involved with their mothers a n d / o r fathers. One boy was so possessed with guilt that h e displaced his aggression for his mother onto another "pussy." He very methodically built gallows and then hanged cats. Of course, it is easy to understand that he was actually killing his mother each time he killed a cat. Another student was a 14 year old girl who had father-daughter relationships over a long period of time. She finally turned her guilt onto herself and tried to eliminate the trauma b y setting herself on fire.

Another student had homosexual incestuous contact with his father. This boy became physically violent and responded by punishing other students by fighting and beating them.

All of these youngsters were from very adequate economic homes. Their parents were all well-educated and held responsible professional positions of work. It is obvious, though, that there was a social-emotional deviation present within each family unit.

The act of i n c e s t , unlike other serious sex crimes, takes place usually within the privacy of the home. Society entrusts the child to the family without obvious supervision, and the only state agency with which the child is required to have contact, is the public school. The sanctity of the home and the right to family privacy are basic to American social and political belief; therefore, in the absence of overt symptoms, family problems remain a family secret. Under these conditions, it is easy to understand why incest cases are rarely discovered.

The following condensed case history illustrates a good example of the kinds of social-sexual deviations that happen within the privacy of one's home:

Q. Has your father ever touched you at any time, in the private areas of your body?

A. Yes.

Q. Can you tell us when and where this happened?

A. It was just before the third grade let out.

Q. In what part of the house did this occur?

A. Mother and Dad's bedroom.

Q. Where was your mother?

A. She was in the room.

Q. What was she doing?

A. Folding up clothes.

Q. Where were you when this happened?

A. On the bed with my father.

Q. What were you wearing?

A. Panties.

Q. Did he remove any of his clothing?

A. No, but he pulled his pajama bottoms down.

Q. Did he remove your clothing?

A. No, but he pulled my pants down.

Q. Did he touch you with his hands?

A. Yes.

Q. What part of his body did he touch you with?

A. (She did not answer, but she pointed to her crotch).

Q. Did he hold you down?

A. Yes.

Q. What did your mother do?

A. She tried to pull him off me.

Q. What did she say?

A. Get off and leave her alone.

Q. What did your father do then?

A. He knocked out two of her front teeth.

Q. What did your mother do then?

A. She kept trying to get him off of me but she could not.

Q. Was your father drunk?

A. I don't know, but he was stumbling around and ran into the door.

Q. What did you do when your father was on top of you?

A. I was crying.

Q. Do you sleep with your parents?

A. Yes.

Q. Did you sleep in the bed with your father while your mother was in the hospital?

A. Yes.

Q. When sleeping with your parents, did you ever see them do what your father was doing to you?

A. Yes.

Q. Has your father ever done anything to you to cause pain besides spanking or whipping?

A. He used his fingers.

Q. Did he put his finger in you?

A. Yes.

Q. Have you ever seen your father bother your brothers in ways similar to the way he bothered you?

A. Yes.

Q. What did he do to R?

A. He made R. put his mouth on it.

Q. When did this happen?

A. I think it was just after R's 10th birthday.

155

Q. Has your father ever done anything like this to you?

A. He put his mouth on me.

Teachers and other adults should be aware of possible behaviors that may help identify a family's life style that stimulates an incestuous environment. These behaviors are somewhat general within homes in which incest is practiced, and your awareness of the following family idiosyncracies may some day help you help a defenseless child:

1. A father whose behavior is characterized by frequent drinking, or by alcoholism; and a history of abusive, unfeeling treatment of other family members.
2. A lack of participation by the father in the dynamics of family life, and over-dependency on him by the mother.
3. The absence of a history of marital relationships, and/or a history of extra-marital relationships.
4. A pattern of rigid, restrictive control by the father of the social life and activities of the female children.
5. Limited contacts with the outside world by the family as a whole and by its individual members.
6. The absence of acting-out behaviors by the children.
7. A large family with many young children.
8. A congested living situation; not enough bedrooms.

Now don't panic and generalize these behaviors to all families. I realize that some of the characteristics are considered within good family relationships and there should be no cause for alarm; but these symptoms do appear to be more evident in family patterns which are incestuous.

KLEPTOMANIA - STEALING

In kleptomania there is a strong and often uncontrollable urge to steal. The behavior is different from ordinary stealing by the fact that the act is impulsive and seemingly without reason. Department store managers, judges, and bewildered parents are faced, from time to time, with habitual stealing by an individual who has been carefully brought up, who is in good financial circumstances, and who does not need what he has stolen.

Kleptomania and shoplifting are different. The shoplifter picks out something he wants to steal, and tries to get away with it before he is caught or forced to pay for the stolen goods. The kleptomaniac may take any article that attracts his attention. He generally does not need the things he steals, and frequently makes no attempt to conceal the fact that he has stolen.

When such people are arrested by store detectives, they are frightened, humiliated, and usually at a loss for an explanation of their strange conduct. All they can say is that the temptation seemed to sweep over them, and that they tried to resist it but felt driven to do it in spite of themselves. Kleptomaniacs say that these impulses and ideas are uncontrollable and force themselves into their minds demanding attention. The will power of the person is usually not strong enough to overcome the demands of the impulses and ideas.

Sex is a factor in a great many cases of compulsive stealing. Kleptomaniacs frequently describe erotic excitement associated with the act of stealing. The individual may steal a wide range of articles but commonly takes more intimate items of women's clothing, particularly panties and brassiers. In some cases the stolen objects are accumulated in a sort of collection. In other s i t u a t i o n s , the person throws them away shortly after the act is completed. The dangerous and forbidden element in such behavior appears to stimulate unconscious fantasies of sexual activities. Sometimes when these individuals are apprehended, they are embarrassed about the stealing impulses and especially about the sexual connotations. Although they do admit freely that they seem unable to help t h e m s e l v e s --that something forced them to perform the act. Fetishism is apparently the basis for many cases of kleptomania. Men, usually young, steal women's wearing apparel from clotheslines and department stores. In some forms of fetishistic behavior, the excitement and suspense involved with stealing the fetishistic object, contributes materially to the sexual excitement.

Compulsive stealing, and the obsessive concern with stealing, have a number of possible explanations. The person who is driven to steal impulsively and without apparent reason may be expressing a reaction against authority. Such behavior is a defiance of the police and the owner of the store, both of whom may represent parental figures.

Inferiority feelings frequently appear as the consequence of a power drive being blocked by parents, or by the habits of thinking established by parental training. Against this parental domination there is rebellion and impulsive irrational activity which may appear in the form of compulsive acts. Frequently instances of kleptomania have been traced to this particular source.

It is possible also that kleptomania may be an expression of a more generalized hostility and aggression within the personality. In some cases, compulsive stealing may be related to a need to defy the accepted way of life by engaging in an activity completely different from the moral and ethical standards under which the person was raised. This type of action also contains elements of hostility.

The need for punishment is an important factor in kleptomania, since most of this type are quickly apprehended. It is as if the person wanted to be caught. At the unconscious level, it may be that certain compulsive neurotics of this kind do in fact have a need to be punished. They may be looking for punishment because of a guilty feeling.

When a person is taken to court for stealing, kleptomania is not regarded as a defense, according to the law. It may be used as a defense if proof can be shown that the kleptomaniac cannot tell right from wrong.

The word "kleptomania" comes from two Greek words meaning "to steal" and "Madness." Kleptomania was once thought to be a form of insanity. But today most psychologists believe that kleptomania is a social disease that can be cured. The kleptomaniac steals to satisfy some deep need in his personality. He can be cured only when the source of this need is understood.

There seems to be some relating behavior between the acts of stealing, fire setting, and wetting or bed-wetting. If you have a child in your home or classroom who is stealing, then I feel that it would be wise to be aware of the possibility that this same child may play with fire. The awareness of any such behavior by a parent or teacher should be to refer a child to a treatment program, because the child will not "grow out of it." He is emotionally sick and he needs help.

PORNOGRAPHY

What is pornography? Sometimes as parents we submit an interpretation of pornography to kids when in reality they may see nothing indicative of dirty sex or even sex. We adults project our own guilts by condemning that which may or may not be bad. It is easy for us as adults to view pictures, movies, read books, and pass our judgements on to others - -youngsters or other adults.

The person who may suddenly find himself crusading to eliminate all dirty movies, magazines, and books, first must see the stock before he can place judgements. He may really be functioning with his own censoring intent to become involved with pornography. That is to say, "I can't morally or conscientiously look at this dirty stuff, but if I look at it as a censor or as a judge for other people, then I am legal." That rationale creates a good defense for one to look, enjoy, and condemn all the bad, bad material.

It seems quite strange that material which will cause parent interest, trauma, and deterioration, never affects the censors. Censors remain pure after they have been exposed to pornography, it is only the average prurient citizen who is corrupted. In his essays on censorship, Francis Bacon expressed similar interpretations, feelings and ambivalences many years ago during William Shakespeare's hay-day. Today we still have the same rationale for censoring.

Many times, that which is forbidden becomes much more interesting and deviant. When things become somewhat common, the mysteries of intent, projection, and evil may disappear.

Again, an example from Wagon Wheel School, we have noticed that some boys who come to the school, have mothers who really get upset when they find a copy of "Playboy" in the boy's bedroom, or a nude picture under his bed or on the wall, or any material suggestive of rotten sex. We tell the boys at Wagon Wheel School, that if he wants to put a single picture on the wall or decorate his room he may do so. Guess what? Invariably he will plaster the walls with nude pictures and as soon as he finds out that nobody is really upset or disturbed, the pictures start coming down, and within a few weeks one probably won't find any more pictures.

The challenge of getting even with or getting back at mom or dad may provide the stimulation for the pictures. Of course, a situation may become circular in which the child gets reference from mom or dad that he is evil and these bad pictures reflect this evil. The child may then be content to agree and really prove he's bad by posting more pictures on the walls.

The evils of pictures, books, or movies may be evil simply because we as adults may express subtle, indirect, or direct, feedback to the youngsters that we do not approve of this trash. The child may have decided for himself that the material is trash; but he must decide, not have mom or dad project their own feelings of evil.

Now, again I'm not saying open the door to filth for your child, but I am saying that we may cause our children to gravitate to our own projected deviations if we don't handle this permissive society with care. So many times, that which is evil, is evil in the eyes of that person only. It is his guilt and anxiety about seeing or reading this trash that is related to the child. Again, let me say that I do not advocate an open door to kids relative to "pornography," but we should be careful not to make a big deal out of something that could easily be digested and discarded by the child.

RUNAWAYS

Terry was the twelve-year-old son of a very successful oil executive. He was a talented musician. He lived in a very large home, complete with swimming pool. He was the proud owner of a motorcycle, and he had run away from home over a hundred times in his young life.

Ann was the daughter of a Southern gentleman. She lived in a mansion of antebellum style. She had her own private maid, her own new car every year, an almost unlimited supply of expense money, and a record of over twenty runaways; the longest distance covered over 1500 miles.

One can hardly pick up a newspaper these days without reading of teenagers whose parents have searched all over the country for some trace of their existence. The classified advertising in such underground newspapers as the "Los Angeles Free Press" and the "Village Voice" are overflowing with pleas from frantic parents and offers of rewards "for information leading to the whereabouts of. . ." A noted detective agency in Dallas, Texas, has related to this writer that ninety percent of their business is involved in searching for adolescent elopements. The glories and hardships of leaving home are discussed in the rock musical, HAIR, and by the Beatles in one of their earlier albums. Running away has become such a problem that many prep-schools, boarding schools, military schools, and other institutions which cater to young people have revised their policies such that running away results in automatic expulsion from the school. This type of ruling has only heightened the incidence of elopement from the school. This type of ruling in institutions such as these are there for disciplinary reasons and this regulation gives them an easy way out of an often uncomfortable situation.

An even sadder element which augments the problems of adolescent runaways is best stated by the old cliche concerning the weather: "Everybody talks about it but nobody does anything about it." This particularly is evident when one begins researching current literature written on this or similar topics. Very little has been written, or if it has been written it is not very well publicized. For this reason it has been necessary to go to the source of the problem in order to attempt to gain information about this syndrome which is sweeping young Americans.

The Wagon Wheel Schools, Inc., a private residential treatment center for emotionally disturbed children, Mc Loud, Oklahoma, provided the population from which the information might be gained. Although the treatment center is coeducational, only adolescent boys were selected for this study. Of the nineteen boys interviewed, fifteen had run away at least once during their young lives.

The group interviewed is small in comparison to the total population of emotionally disturbed male adolescents, consequently, there is no basis for the information noted in the following pages to be generalized to the population as a whole; however at the very least, a great deal is brought out which provides a basis for surmisal, hypothesis, and concerned pondering.

The group was polled as to how many had experienced at least one runaway, either from home, from Wagon Wheel, or from another school, treatment center or hospital. Fifteen of the nineteen responded affirmatively. It was then explained that the writer would present them with a questionnaire to complete on each runaway, that this was completely voluntary, and that the questionnaires would be anonymous. The only identifying information on a form would be the sex of the individual (this was placed on the questionnaire form prior to a decision to delete the study of female adolescent runaways) and the month and year of his birth.

Reassurance was needed prior to commencement, that the writer would not check the dates of birth with their own files, nor would any of this information be related to the Wagon Wheel Chief of Staff; a child psychiatrist in charge of t r e a t m e n t for the majority of the students.

All of the students then agreed to complete the questionnaire forms. The shortest time utilized for this purpose was twelve minutes and the greatest amount of time taken was one hour and seventeen minutes. Observation of the behavior of the students during this time confirmed an a i r of seriousness and determination in completion of the forms. G e n e r a l comments ranged from, "I really didn't consider this a runaway at the time, but I guess I'll go ahead and tell about it anyway," to "Jim, do you remember what month it was that you bailed me out of detention in Norman?"

Judging from overall appearances of the entire group, all students were objective and forthright in their responses.

SAMPLE QUESTIONNAIRE

Date of birth_____

Sex_____

1. This was my _____runaway. (1st, 2nd, 10th)
2. How old were you at the time of this runaway?
3. From where did you run away?
4. What time of the day or night did you leave?
5. In what month did you leave?
6. Were you alone or with others?
7. Did you plan the runaway or were you asked to go with someone else?

8. Was the runaway planned in advance or an on-the-spot decision?
9. Where did you intend to go?
10. How far was this from your starting point?
11. Where did you go?
12. How far was this from your starting point?
13. How did you plan to travel?
14. What was your method of travel?
15. Why did you return?
16. If you were picked up by the police, how did they treat you?
17. How do you think your parents reacted when they learned you were gone.
18. How did your parents react when you returned?
19. What were the consequences of your runaway?
20. How long were you gone?
21. Why did you run away?

Note: Appropriate spaces were provided on the original questionnaire form to allow space to answer.

Fifteen adolescent boys completed questionnaire forms concerning their runaway experiences. The ages of these boys ranged from fourteen years, ten months, to nineteen years, three months. In all, a total of forty-one runaways were reported. This included five students who had run away one time, five students who had run away two times, two students who had run away three times, one student who had run away four times, one student who had run away seven times, and one who had run away nine times.

An interesting pattern is instantly noted when the ages of the students at the time of their first runaway are considered. Five of the boys experienced their first runaway at either age seven or eight. Then there was a period of three years, ages nine, ten, and eleven, completely free from runaway activity. Two report their first runaway was at the age of twelve, no one at age thirteen, and one experienced his at age fourteen. Here we see a period of six years, half of a child's public education life, with only twenty per cent of the students choosing that time for their first runaway experience. Yet, over thirty-three per cent of the boys initiated their elopement activity at the age of seven or eight.

As might be expected, the ages which correspond to high school attendance account for almost fifty per cent of the initial runaways, three at the age of fifteen, two at age sixteen, and two at seventeen.

In noting a graphic illustration of this information we are able to see that the trend definitely leans toward either very young experiences or late adolescent elopement. This trend can be developed a bit farther by noting the reasons for leaving and the length of time gone in each age group.

Our youngest beginner started his career as a runner at age seven because he "couldn't stand the maid." He was a bit unsuccessful in his attempt in that he was only ten minutes departed when the hated maid foiled his attempt. The four who first ran at age eight were similar to each other in that there was a sort of instant anger which precipitated the elopements. They are also similar in that the length of time gone ranged from ten minutes to four hours.

Likewise, the seven students who ran away for the first time at age fifteen, sixteen, or seventeen, recorded similarities in noting reasons for elopement. The most prevalent reason noted was in some form concerned with their attempts to get out from under parental control. Other reasons ranged from "just wanted a vacation," to what has to be considered the most creative reason given, even though it might be lack-

ing a bit in veracity: "We went on an expedition following the river bed from the trash dump, and studied
flora and fauna along the way. When we returned, it
was an absolute shock to know that we had run away
and were listed as "runaways', although nobody knew
that we had run at the time, until we were seen walking up the road, I think."

In response to question three, eleven responded
that they ran away from home the first time while four
eloped from school. This figure becomes a bit more
even when the total number of runaways is considered,
because twenty-one of the runaways were from home and
twenty from school or other origins.

A particularly interesting facet comes to light
in studying this problem through analyzing individual
cases. For instance, the young man with the greatest
number (9) of elopements, ran away from home the first
five times. The next four times he ran, he was run-
ing from Wagon Wheel School to his home. This pattern
is similar to that reported by many of the other students who reported multiple runaways. This tendency
appears to correlate with the psychological evaluations of most of the students who have run away.

Prior to studying the results of the questionnaires, it was firmly entrenched in my mind that the
great majority of all runaways occur very late in the
evening. In defining the time for our purposes, from
6:00 am until noon comprise the morning hours. Afternoon takes in the next hours until 6:00 pm, and night
refers to all hours from 6:00 pm until 6:00 am. Com-
bining, therefore, the double amount of time at night
with the minimum of supervision that occurs during
these hours, it is somewhat surprising to learn that
less than forty-seven percent of the runaways occurred

during this time. Forty-one percent of the runaways commenced between the hours of noon and 6:00 pm.

It appears that there is no real preference as to the time of the year to the run-away. Twenty-two percent of the runaways happened in the spring, thirty-two percent in the summer, seventeen percent in the fall, fourteen percent in the winter, and the remainder were unable to remember in what month they left.

Another preconceived idea was in reference to Question six, "Were you alone or with others?" No significant pattern was established by any of the respondents. As a matter of fact, of the fifteen first elopements, seven were undertaken alone and eight were in the company of others or another. The difference is the same when the total number of runaways is considered. Twenty of the elopements were solitary while twenty-one were with others.

In reply to Question seven, only one person admitted to being asked to go with another group on his first runaway. The other fourteen stated that it was their own idea to run, that they were the planners of the operation. Sixty percent of the boys stated that their first runaway was the result of a spur-of-the-moment decision rather than a planned ordeal.

An interesting correlation arises concerning Questions ten and twelve. It would be surmised that a good deal of the time the intended distance would be somewhat shorter than the distance actually accomplished, and this is the case. However, more pertinent is the comparison of the intended destination of the boys' first runaway with their most recent elopement. Ten of the students stated that their destination when they first ran away was less than one hundred miles from their starting point. Two boys related that they had no particular destination in mind. Comparing this with the eleven most recent runaways, seven persons stated that their intended destinations ranged f r o m one hundred to five hundred miles.

Success in reaching their goals was much higher on the first runaways; however, twelve of the fifteen students reached their intended destinations. The eleven most recent runaways were successful in only four cases, with five of the persons planning trips of one hundred to five hundred miles actually traveling less than ten miles.

By far the most popular method of travel was either on foot, hitchhiking, or a combination of the two. The o n l y other methods mentioned throughout the forty-one cases reported were by bus and with friends in their cars.

Police involvement in the elopements did not appear to be a factor. Only eight r u n a w a y s were picked up by the police. The comments on how they were treated ranged from "like a criminal," to "very nicely," with the majority leaning toward the latter. As a deterrent, police involvement might be considered a failure. Only three of the eight arrested refrained from running again after their being picked up. The others ran from one to eight times more after their involvement with the law.

Nearly all the boys were able to diagnose the feelings of their parents both prior to and upon their return. Comments ranged from, "They were very worried when they learned I had gone and pleased when I returned," to "Very shocked when they learned of my absence and very nice immediately after my return and cruel soon after."

It was thought by this writer that Question twenty-one, "Why did you run away?" and Question nineteen, "What were the consequences of your runaway?" would provide the most revealing information gathered from this questionnaire. The responses to Question twenty-one were very patternistic with regard to the age at the time of the runaway and the present day adolescent ideology. Freedom from the supervision of parents, counselors, teachers, or other authority figures was the primary cause in the fifteen-seventeen year old runaways, while anger toward parents or playmates constituted the major reasoning behind the younger elopements.

Five different methods of punishment were noted as having been used by parents when the students ran away from home. Whipping and spanking were the most frequent, being used in seven different instances. Grounding the student or placing him on some type of restriction accounted for four instances, as did verbal admonishings, preachings, etc. Three of the parents sent their sons away to boarding schools or treatment centers as a result of running away, while six runaways ended up with no consequences whatsoever.

The effectiveness of these various methods might be measured in the following way: The first runaway experience of the fifteen boys was considered along with their method of punishment. We then noted the number of subsequent elopements made by those students who were involved in each method of punishment. The figures are as follows: Four students were spanked after their first runaway. These four students participated in a total of sixteen runaways following this punishment. Three students were grounded after their first experience, and they ran a total of three times after that. Only one student was sent away to a boarding school after his first runaway, and he has eloped three times since then. Two were only scolded following their first runaways and there has been only one run since that time. No consequences were dealt upon three of the boys after their first times of running, and a total of two elopements have transpired between the three since that time. The remaining two students ran away from a school their first time and work was administered as their punishment. Since that time, only one boy has attempted a subsequent run.

Although these figures are quite inconclusive, it is apparent that in the case of these fifteen adolescent boys, s p a n k i n g was the lease effective d e t e r r e n t, while work, restricting, scolding and school placement are about as effective as doing nothing. The runaway profiles are illustrated in the following tables.

Table 3:   Overview of Subjects Questioned

Subject	Age	No. of Runaways
1	15-8	9
2	19-0	7
3	16-11	4
4	16-8	3
5	16-7	3
6	16-8	2
7	18-3	2
8	16-8	2
9	15-1	2
10	17-10	2
11	19-3	1
12	17-9	1
13	17-7	1
14	17-10	1
15	14-10	1

Table 4: Ages of students at the time of the first runaway.

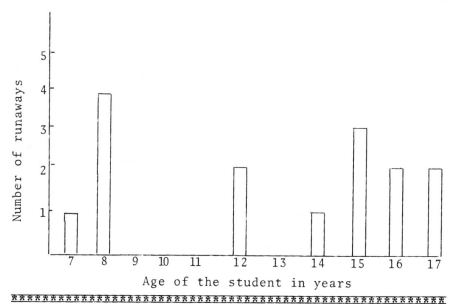

Age of the student in years

✕✕

Table 5: Number of runaways reported per year, 1959-70.

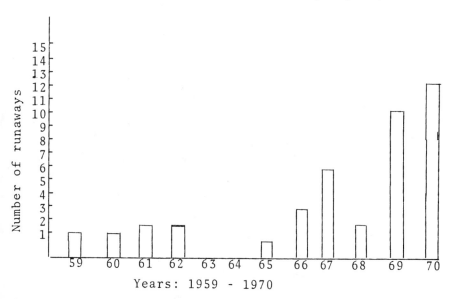

Years: 1959 - 1970

173

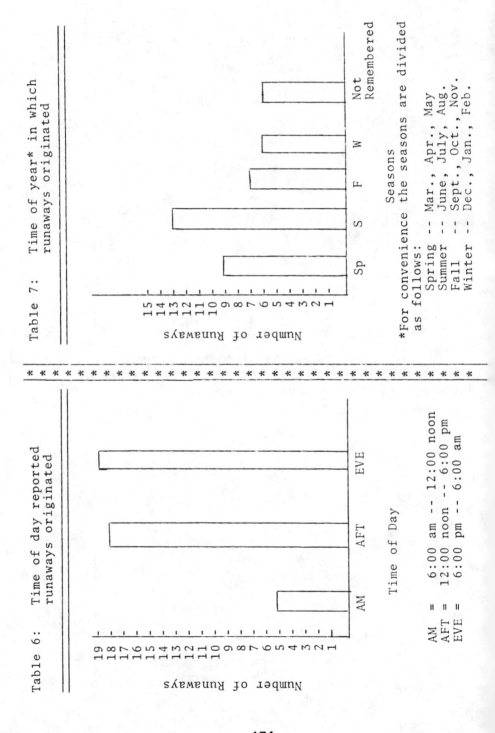

Table 7: Time of year* in which runaways originated

Number of Runaways

Sp   S   F   W   Not Remembered

Seasons

*For convenience the seasons are divided as follows:

Spring -- Mar., Apr., May.
Summer -- June, July, Aug.
Fall   -- Sept., Oct., Nov.
Winter -- Dec., Jan., Feb.

Table 6: Time of day reported runaways originated

Number of Runaways

AM   AFT   EVE

Time of Day

AM = 6:00 am -- 12:00 noon
AFT = 12:00 noon -- 6:00 pm
EVE = 6:00 pm -- 6:00 am

174

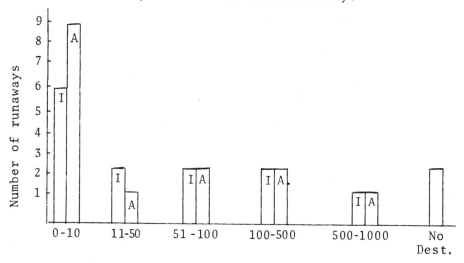

Table   8: Intended distance and distance
            actually achieved on first runaway.

DISTANCE IN MILES

I = Intended Distance
A = Achieved Distance

****

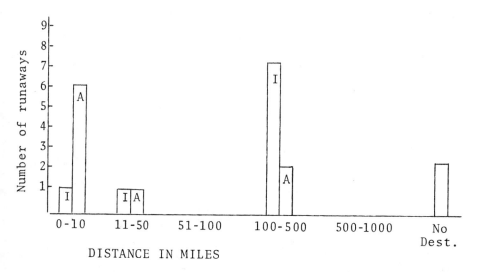

Table   9: Intended distance and distance actually
            achieved on most recent runaway.

DISTANCE IN MILES

I = Intended Distance
A = Achieved Distance

175

Table 10: Types of Punishment Used by Parents

Type of Punishment	No. of times used
Spanking	7
Restriction of privileges or movement	4
Removal from home situation and placement in boarding school	3
Scolding	4
No punishment	6

****

Table 11: Effectiveness of different types of punishment as a deterrent of subsequent runaways

Type of Punishment	No. of times used	No. of subsequent runaways
Spanking	4	16
Restriction	3	3
Scolding	2	1
School Placement	1	3
Work	2	1
No Punishment	3	2

Information for this study was provided by Jim Maley, Director of Wagon Wheel Schools, Inc., Mc Loud, Oklahoma, Mr. and Mrs. Bob Daugherty, Founders and Owners.

SUICIDE

Recent statistics have shown a steady increase in suicides among children and adolescents in the United States. This is an alarming fact to many adults particularly to those individuals who are directly involved in dealing with this age group. The study of this increasing problem certainly should m e r i t a substantial amount of research in depth. However, to the writer's chagrin, it appears th a t very little interest has been shown with regard to this problem.

The stigma society attaches to suicide in general may be a very important factor contributing to this seeming lack of interest. M a r g u e r i t e Clark (1961) quotes Dr. Leif J. Braaten as saying, "Suicide, particularly in the young, is c o n s i d e r e d a taboo subject for the lay public, and even professional people are sometimes reluctant to d i s c u s s or study the problem."

It is because of this same stigma that the statistics on childhood and adolescent suicide cannot be considered entirely reliable. Many suicides are never recorded as such because of the efforts of ashamed parents, well-meaning friends and relatives, or sympathetic physicians. There is some indication that ten to fifteen percent o f accidents, particularly home accidents are actually suicides.

The need for better understanding of t h i s problem is quite evident. Although there may be no specific way to prevent all childhood and adolescent suicides, an effort should be made to become acquainted with some of the indications and possible causes of potential suicide in the hope that it may be averted to some extent.

I should like to consider some of the common misconceptions about suicide. "Children who verbalize the threat to commit suicide rarely do." This is one of the most commonly held misconceptions about suicide. An estimate as high as eighty per cent of the children and adolescents who do take their lives have mentioned suicide previous to the act.

"Children who kill themselves are insane." A psychotic condition is not always present in suicide. Although this may be the case in some suicides, the majority of the children and teenagers would not be considered mentally ill. There is some degree of emotional disturbance, of course, but not to the extent of psychosis.

"Children commit suicide without warning." Suicide does not happen quickly, with no previous clues as to what may occur. According to Marguerite Clark, (1961), "Weeks, months, or even years of struggle between the death wish and the natural instinct to live and enjoy life usually precede the child's attempt to do away with himself."

Presuicidal hints can usually be detected by trained individuals. This detection may be somewhat less effective with regard to adolescents. Many teenagers appear to kill themselves for seemingly trivial reasons and with very little forewarning. However, in most instances, there is usually an underlying emotional problem of great intensity.

"The tendency to commit suicide is inherited." This is a fallacy which is believed by many people, even in this enlightened age of 1974. Although the tendency itself is not inherent, some authorities feel that in some instances suicidal children may identify with a parent or relative who has committed suicide.

An observation of suicide factual evidence , indicates that the rate of suicide among children and adolescents is increasing. There is an apparent 25 percent rate of increase in the past ten years.

More boys than girls are successful in committing suicide; even though statistics show that more girls make the attempt. However, this has not always been true. Louis I. Dublin (1963) states that in the earlier decades of this century, the rate of suicide among girls was significantly higher than that of boys. This rate has steadily decreased over the past half century by three-fourths, while the rate for boys has remained fairly stable. The total amount of teen-age suicides may appear to be relatively small in comparison to the total number of suicides in the United States each year. However, the number of suicide attempts made by this age group represents a much larger figure to be considered.

Karl Menninger (1938) states that there are three basic components involved in suicide: (1) the wish to kill, (2) the wish to be killed, and (3) the wish to die. Menninger feels that these elements are present in all suicides, although in varying degrees.

Probably one of the most prevalent causes of suicides among children and adolescents is that of a cry for help. The individual may feel that he faces a serious dilemma and for all intents and purposes can find no avenue of communication by which he may express his conflict. Reverend Kenneth B. Murphy, (1965) has stated, "In the child's desperate attempt to convey those circumstances which beset him, there cannot be placed too much importance on the ultimate value of the need to be heard and understood."

Another cause of suicide is the need to punish others. This need often expresses feelings of anger, hate, and revenge. In studying suicide notes left by children and teenagers, some authorities have found evidence of all these feelings. The very fact that children and teenagers, particularly teenagers, leave notes is in itself a clue to the individual's desire for the survivors to realize how he feels toward them.

This cause also finds expression in the common childhood fantasy of dying as a means of punishing parents. The typical remark, "If I were dead (or killed), they'd be sorry for what they did," is an example of this wish.

Ignorance of the finality of death is also a cause of suicide, particularly among children. At this age children are not intellectually prepared to handle death in a realistic manner and very few young children have a true realization of what death actually entails. Suicidal children may have the mistaken idea that by taking their own lives, "Everything will come out all right and so will I." Reverend Murphy (1965) thinks, "The feeling of the child himself is generally that he will survive after death." This ignorance may be because of the way in which adults explain death to children. Or it may be explained by the fact that they see actors on television killed one night and alive on another program the next night.

A fourth cause of childhood and adolescent suicide may be the urge to repent for some sin. This may entail all types of real or imagined reasons: Everything from the failure to care properly for a pet to severe sexual anxieties. However, it must be noted that although these "sins" may seem real to the suicidal victim, most of them seem rather trivial upon investigation.

Another cause of suicide may be the loss of status. This cause seems to be the more prevalent in adolescent rather than childhood suicides. It occurs when an individual can no longer handle the discrepency between how he appears to himself and how he desires to be. Loss of status is also operating in the situation of parents who continuously demand behavior which the child is incapable of performing.

Reaction to a family death may be a cause of suicide among children and adolescents. The individual may be identifying with a parent or relative who has recently died. He may have a strong desire to be reunited with the lost love object and may feel that suicide is the most immediate way in which to fulfill this wish. Or the victim may feel that suicide would provide the ultimate escape from an intolerable loss.

Still another cause of childhood and adolescent suicide is mental illness. However, as I mentioned previously, this is not a major cause. Emotional disturbance to some degree is present in suicidal victims, but psychosis is not necessarily a prerequisite for suicide. A very paranoid person may destroy himself, because he will attempt to remove the persecution he personally feels by either destroying those whom he believes are picking on him, or by destroying himself. Either way, he is successful in stopping the persecution.

The child or adolescent who talks about suicide is exhibiting a great tendency toward the act. This verbalization of a threat is probably the most important clue to a potential suicide. Suicide victims have proven that most individuals who have intellectualized and talked about suicide are usually the ones who attempt to destroy themselves. Another important clue as to a potential suicide is the child or teenager who discusses another person's death frequently. This preoccupation with the death of a relative or another individual with whom the child may identify can signify a definite tendency toward suicide.

A previous attempt at suicide is most certainly a danger signal. The number of false suicide attempts is almost nonexistent. Many unconscious suicide attempts are made by youngsters who indulge in drag racing, reckless skiing, risky swims without training or supervision. Behind this daring is a death wish.

Sudden changes in the personality or behavior of a child or adolescent may be a clue to potential suicide. Neglect of personal appearance in a child who is usually well-groomed may also signal a disturbance which could result in suicide. A youngster who suddenly loses all interest in studies, sports, or hobbies that once were very important to him, may be exhibiting signs of conflict which could be responsible, ultimately, for suicide. Other changes in behavior, such as the child who is normally outgoing becoming secretive and withdrawn; or the child who begins acting out quite negatively, may be hints of problems that may result in suicide. Nailbiting, nervous tics, stuttering, and other speech difficulties may also provide clues;but these should be considered in relation to other changes in the overall pattern of behavior.

In summary, I must say that suicide is probably one of the least understood forms of withdrawal. The tragedy of such an attempt to withdraw, is that a person may easily become a permanent statistic. There are many pseudo concepts relative to a suicide attempt--"He just wants attention. He really doesn't want to die. Those who talk about it will never attempt suicide, etc." Maybe truth, maybe fiction, but one fact does remain, regardless of the motive for the attempt, if there is no one around to save the person, it may become a very fatal attempt.

If you tell a potential suicidal person that he is only seeking attention and he really won't kill himself, you will probably not deter his action. Your attention may instead propell his action to a more intense level. Have you ever tried talking with a person who has threatened suicide? If you have, you realize that it is a pretty hopeless conversation. He will not listen to logic or reason. He cannot give you a well defined reason for wanting to die. He will not heed your commands or your requests. He seems only more intent upon his efforts to destroy himself. He didn't really plan to do it, a mistake, attention; no matter what you call it, the result is still death.

Years ago, I had a young girl, 15 years old, in a high school class. I saw her in the hallway during a class period and asked her where she should be, and she replied very happily with a big smile, "Oh, I've just taken some lotion and I will kill myself." She was laughing and showing no expression of concern. I jokingly said, "Yes, sure, blah, blah, blah." She left and I went to the nurse's office, and twenty minutes later we found her in a broom closet. She was taken to the doctor. He pumped her stomach; and sure enough, she had taken a lethal dose.

LESSON: If a child talks death, suicide, let that talk serve as a warning, because the child who talks about suicide is the one who will attempt it. The person who has an abortive attempt will be the one who will try again and again; and some day there will be no one near enough to help him, and he will die. You can't force counseling onto a person, but you can open your doors and listen to them and not call him a phony attention seeker.

We had a 13 year old boy at Wagon Wheel School, McLoud, Oklahoma, a couple of years ago, who came to us with chronic suicide attempts. This boy had tried many different ways to kill himself, but someone was always there to save him. After a year or so he began to respond extremely well in therapy. One night another boy attempted suicide, so we thought we would have boy (1) talk to boy (2) and tell him how he felt, and all the ridiculousness that went along with the attempts that he had made on his life. We felt that with his experience, he could talk to the other boy and perhaps get through to him. When we asked boy (1) to talk to boy (2) he said, "You know, I can't remember how I felt then: it doesn't seem as though it ever happened. I just can't talk to the other boy and tell him anything." This boy's suicide attempts, thoughts of death, and self-destruction were gone, and he could not recall the trauma that was involved. He does remember that his past attempts were real and that he

184

felt badly enough to destroy himself, but he was unable to relate anything to detour the number (2) boy's attempt.

Open your door and your heart, don't try to tell the person that he's not serious, that he really doesn't want to kill himself. He may just do it and prove you wrong. Listen to him if he wishes to talk to you, but don't censor, judge, or blame him. Try to let him know that someone cares, that one person really cares.

Suicide is the second leading killer of young people. Only one thing, accidents kill more teenagers than does suicide, and I feel quite sure that many accidents--good swimmer drowns in two feet of water, one car accidents, etc.--are probably suicide attempts not accidents. Listen, parents and teachers, and take heed if a child emits warning signals. Remember, he who talks about destroying himself is a good candidate to attempt suicide. If you become aware of only one child in your lifetime who expresses self-destruction tendencies, and you are able to attend to the child, then this dialogue will have served a life saving mission.

REFERENCES

Clark, Marguerite, "Children in the Dark," Parent-Teacher Association Magazine, LV (May, 1961).

Dublin, Louis I., Suicide : A Sociological and Statistical Study, New York: The Ronald Press Co., 1963.

Menninger, Karl A. Man Against Himself, New York: Harcourt, Brace and Co., 1938.

Murphy, Kenneth B., "Do They Really Want to Die?" Today's Health, XLIII (April, 1965).

SECTION THREE

INTELLECTUAL BEHAVIOR

The first concern of educating the gifted child
is one of identification.   Usually, the bright or
gifted child is easy to spot by judging the performance of his work, but too often gifted children with
high IQ's and other high potentialities are overlooked by the classroom teacher because they don't pay
close attention in class or perhaps because they are
a little rowdy.

Classroom teachers in the past have been the
main source of identification of the gifted child.
(This is being replaced by standard tests of mental
ability.)   Many times the teacher will select those
students as gifted children, who are obedient, well-
dressed, well-groomed, and readily conform to classroom procedure.   This procedure can be a tragic
mistake on the part of the teacher. Many gifted or
creative children who learn rapidly and easily become
bored with rote-learning drills.   If the gifted child
has already learned his multiplication tables; he
derives no further benefit from continuous practice
in rote learning drills. Consequently, losing the
challenge, he loses interest and may become rowdy or
disturbing to the rest of the classroom. He may rush
through the drills haphazardly and make several careless mistakes, thus lowering his grades.

Those children who learn quickly and become
bored while waiting on the rest of the class, are the
ones the teacher might possibly categorize as problem
children.   To counteract this possibility, teachers
have been provided with information and lists of
characteristics to help them identify a child with

high mental ability. One such list of characteristics is cited below, (Gallagher, 1964):

1. Learns rapidly and easily.
2. Uses a lot of common sense and practical knowledge.
3. Reasons things out, thinks clearly, recognizes relationships, comprehends meanings.
4. Retains what he has heard or read without much rote drill.
5. Knows about many things of which other children are unaware.
6. Uses a large number of words easily and accurately.
7. Can read books that are one to two years in advance of the rest of the class.
8. Performs difficult mental tasks,
9. Asks many questions. Is interested in a wide range of things.
10. Does some academic work one to two years in advance of the class.
11. Is alert, keenly observant, responds quickly.

Giftedness, particularly in childhood, usually means greatly advanced development for one's own life age. If a teacher is to be able to identify correctly children who fall in this category; she must first know what the expectations of intellectual performance are at given age levels.

Because of the difficulties in teacher nomination of the gifted, standardized tests for mental ability are becoming more widely used. These intelligence tests, also have their limitations. One of the basic difficulties is that the IQ test does not appear to measure the entire area of intellect. By using the IQ test score as the only measure of giftedness, the educational system runs the risk of overlooking children whose creative abilities might be very high, but whose abilities measured by their IQ scores might be only moderate.

Another limitation of the IQ test is its dependence on the student's reading skill. The child who cannot read r a p i d l y may be handicapped on group IQ tests. Group intelligence tests are sometimes good for screening, but they often d o not identify those students who may h a v e emotional problems or lack of motivation. One means of counteracting this omission is the individual intelligence test, which is by f a r the best method o f identification; b u t it is expensive relative to professional time and services. Two other tests which should be used with the intelligence tests a re achievement test batteries, and creative ability tests. These tests will possibly i d e n tify talented or gifted children who did not show u p a s being exceptional on the IQ tests.

None of the identification m e tho d s of gifted children are without flaws. In reality then, a combination of the v a r i o u s procedures including teacher observation, g r o u p intelligence tests, i n d i v idual intelligence tests, aptitude tests, creativity tests, and leadership tests, would provide a more thorough answer to the problem of identification. Identification, however, is only the first step. Some kind of action or educational program must follow to develop the p o tentialities of these children to their fullest extent. It is the school's business to recognize and develop talent whether or not parents take any responsibility. The school is the major community institution w h e r e gifted children may find help. As such, it has a m a jor responsibility to society. (DeHaan; Havighurst,'61)

After identification of the gifted child, under-achievement becomes of major importance. A child has b e e n identified as gifted. Why doesn't he produce accordingly? Why does one child fail to develop his abilities and another seem to r e a c h the top? These are questions m a n y teachers are faced with. There are no definite, concrete answers. The underachiever is the person who does not fulfill himself. In academic terms, he is generally defined a s the student whose achievement is markedly inferior t o his tested intellectual ability, (Gold, 1965).

Several studies a n d investigations of the negative attitudes o f the underachieving s t u d e n t have indicated a direct relationship between the negative attitudes and family attitudes and values. Gallagher, 1964, c i t e s one such study by Pierce and Bowman i n which they found that high achieving students believed their fathers were more important influences in their lives than d i d low achievers. The low achievers usually chose some male figure (an uncle, m i n i s t e r , or teacher) outside the family as the most important influence on their lives. The fathers of the under-achievers usually showed more hostility and rejection than did the fathers of the overachievers. The mothers of underachievers a l s o seemed to differ significantly from the mothers in families where the youngster was performing effectively. One study indicated that the mothers of h i g h achieving boys were l o we r in authoritarianism t h a n were the m o t h e r s of low achieving boys.

What has happened in the lives of many o f these underachieving youngsters i s a failure t o identify with the parent of the same sex; thus failing to introject, or take into one's self the values and attitudes of that parent. When a n y child, not necessarily the gifted child, cannot properly identify w i t h adults because the model i s unacceptable to them for various reasons; they find other models of behavior. These outside models are usually peer groups who band together with other dissatisfied youngsters.

The underachiever has a somewhat asocial personality and is rejecting s c h o o l as part of his total pattern of rejection of the values of society. Underachievers feel rejected by their families and in turn reject their families and their f a m i l i e s ' values. T h e y are also r e l u c t a n t to accept the values of society.

Low aspirations are characteristic of the underachiever. A l s o , when the underachiever no longer believes in himself, he a d o p t s a belief in fate or luck, or rather bad luck. These attitudes and values which differentiate the achiever from the underachiever have been present from an early age. Self-ratings of the individuals and r a t i n g s by other interested persons seem generally to agree on four major characteristics differentiating these underachieving i n di-viduals from effective achievers:

1. Lack of self-confidence
2. The inability to persevere
3. A lack of integration to goals
4. The presence of inferiority feelings.

The rejection of family values, social v a l u e s , a n d attitudes in underachievers is a characteristic, predominantly found in the m i d d l e -class family and background. Their underachievement consists to some extent, of revolt against the attitudes and values of that class. Another cause for underachievement rapidly coming t o the forefront is cultural deprivation. The social e n v i r o n m e n t and background in which a child grows, plays a n important role in the development of any potential talent he may possess.

Many children in families of lower socioeconomic status fail to develop their abilities because of lack of opportunity and stimulation from their earliest years. Why this lack of opportunity or more importantly, why the lack of stimulation? These children come from homes where they are not encouraged to read, learn music, draw pictures, develop scientific hobbies, or even advance themselves in education at all. In these families, education is not an important aspect of life. The family is usually struggling for survival, and when a child of this lower-status family reaches high school, he is pressured to work and earn money to help the family income. He gets little financial aid from home, and in all probability will find it difficult to get a scholarship that would take him through college or even through a program of special training. Our colleges in awarding scholarships, tend to favor the middle-class child from the low-income family who needs the scholarship more, (DeHaan, 1961).

If we review the many studies of production of talent from different segments of our society, we find that the principle areas where talent exists but has not been fully developed are as follows:

1. Families of low socioeconomic status. Negroes are the principle group of this area. Minority ethnic groups are also underproductive of talent.
2. Rural areas.
3. Among females.

In economic studies and follow-up studies of children from lower socioeconomic classes, four behavior patterns exist which predispose the individual either favorably or unfavorably toward education. These four patterns are the middle class, the matriarchy, the gang, and the nuclear family.

If the individual's identification is with the middle class, he will probably accept the values held by that class and will view education as an important aspect of his life. He is striving to step up from his lower-class status. In this case his commitment to middle-class status even takes precedence over earlier religious, family, or political affiliations.

A second pattern, however, discovered in the lower-class families is the matriarch. In this pattern of behavior, the mother and daughter take sides against the rest of the world. Men are seldom viewed in a favorable light. This negative attitude toward men is often transferred to male members of that family which results in the alienation of the son from his mother. The dependence which this system stimulates is not conducive to the development of independent thinking.

A masculine equivalent condition that is forced into existence by the matriarchy, is the gang. Formed by teenage young men, the gang is a retreat for aggressive independence from the matriarchy. It provides an aura of secrecy which excludes female membership, and it provides a grandeur display of virility. The chief goal for the gang, is complete independence from responsibility and matriarchal domination.

Since educational achievement is believed to be a feminine characteristic, a teacher, particularly a female teacher, with a boy in her class who has grown up in this type of environment, may more easily understand his underachievement. If she asks him to pay more attention to his school work; she is, in a sense, asking him to give up part of his masculinity. One way to improve this situation would be to have an extremely masculine teacher; thus creating the image that achievement and learning need not be identified solely as feminine characteristics.

The fourth behavior pattern found in the lower-socioeconomic class is one of the nuclear family. In this pattern, family unity is the main objective. If higher education is going to take the child out of the family unit and put him in a different culture, then education as a whole will be discouraged and rejected by the family.

Underachievers in the rural areas can be grouped with underachievers from low socioeconomic areas, in respect to cultural deprivation. Many of the facilities and opportunities for developing potential giftedness are not available in the rural areas. Nor are the encouragement and ambition for achievement in education found in the rural areas in great quantities.

Underachievement among girls is largely because of social institutionalization. For generations the feminine role has been taught as being less aggressive than the masculine role. Aggression and achievement are characteristics of the masculine role. The woman has been taught that to be feminine, she must not wish or strive for as great achievement as a man would. Society still looks skeptically at the woman who excels in a field normally thought to be male territory.

The gifted students listed as underachievers because of cultural deprivation, particularly those from the lower socioeconomic class, are not rebelling against parental pressure. They simply live in a climate where achievement is not the desired norm. The negative reaction of these talented youths stems from a reality. Opportunities for advancement through academic channels are limited to youngsters in minority groups.

Where does the inspiration come from? How do we motivate this portion of the population to strive for achievement? How do we change the values and attitudes and the expected norms of past decades?

"Motivation may best be described as an internal response to some stimulus situation, which in turn serves as a stimulus to action," (Cruickshank, 1969). If we view motives as such, we note that one could change another's motives by changing that individual's perception of a situation. Motives could also be changed by conditioning--by altering the initial association or response to the prescribed stimulus. One could conceive the idea of changing a child's motivation by altering his environment--by changing his home attitudes. The important thing, however, in motivation is not to manipulate the environment as much as it is to help the individual see himself and his world more positively. The key to the individual's behavior is in his immediate perception of a situation and his self concept, (Gold, 1965).

Parents can make a major contribution by providing a rich and stimulating environment which supports the child's ideas and doesn't threaten his security. Children who are anxiety-free have a better chance at developing the ability for clear thinking and mastering a wider variety of intellectual tasks. Every child should be read to by either his parents or other adults. He needs to be taught

stories, songs, and how to play games. He needs
toys that invite both mental and physical motor development. He needs a varied assortment of experiences such as going to the zoo, feeding the animals,
a walk in the park, museums, a trip downtown, bus
trips, etc. He should be supplied with paint,
crayons, paper, puzzles, and other creative toys.
All these tools will condition or stimulate the child.
If read to, the child may want to learn to read himself. He soon may want to be able to do all these
things for himself. The home environment can encourage the gifted child without forcing him. There is
no need to pressure the child into achieving these
tasks. Offering the child encouragement and providing him with easy access to materials is a stimulus
in itself.

The home environment also provides the background for the child's social development. The parents
can help by accepting the responsibility of providing
the facilities for social interaction--by supervising
play relationships--by teaching the child to get
along with other children. Parents can encourage
their child to join different social groups and hobby
clubs. All these social interactions provide the
child with an assortment of experiences which guide
him toward his own decisions in interaction with
other people.

The home environment, too, provides the most
immediate example. If the child sees his parents
interacting in mature, social relationships; he will
have a better understanding or insight into his own
relationships. The home environment, however, is
not the only source of influence on the child. The

school plays an important role also. How the school approaches the child, and how the t e a c h e r conducts her classroom are important factors in stimulating the child.

Considerable research has shown that teachers have a g r e a t e r impact on the aspirations of their students when the students i d e n t i f i e d with and wanted to be like the teachers. Students were more w i l l i n g to raise their aspirations when they felt the teacher was being fair with them. They were willing to work harder if the goal were within reach. Schools can provide contact and interaction with various professions. By contact with these different professions , some of the students will identify with these various people and aspire to be like them. The school should also consider selecting teachers who feel a great need for compatible achievement and a sense of accomplishment. These teachers will have a similar influence on their students. Their enthusiasm will carry over to some of the children.

The s c h o o l also should provide the service of counseling. Group counseling has been recommended for use with gifted adolescents. It is felt that in this way, they appreciate the opportunity to exchange ideas with peers. Also they seem to be reassured to find other persons of t h e i r own age having problems similar to their own.

F a m i l y counseling has also been experimented with to some extent. In this technique the parents and the child are seen t o g e t h e r by the counselor. Usually for the first few sessions, though, the student will see the counselor with a different set of parents other than his own. This gives him the opportunity of getting used to discussing his problems with adults and listening to the adult point of view without being emotionally connected. After the students can talk freely in front of adults; their own parents are brought into the sessions. The main advantage of this type of counseling is that the students feel honored to be allowed to discuss their problems on an equal level with adults.

Stimulation of the culturally deprived gifted child poses an entirely different type of problem for the school, yet the objectives are essentially the same. The predominant attempt should be to provide the child with enriching experiences not found in the home, by widening the cultural field of the student. The premise is that exposure to cultural experiences or adventures of the mind will change the motivation of the culturally deprived child and raise his level of aspirations. The curriculum goal should be to widen the students' cultural perspective. This could be done by attendance at concerts, plays, museums, libraries, and college functions, (Gallagher, 1964).

Stimulation of culturally deprived children may well prove to be the most difficult task attempted by our present-day educational system. Teaching these children and trying to change their attitudes and increase their motivation is made more difficult by the lack of encouragement and negative attitudes toward education found in their homes. The major question, and answer, to motivation of the culturally deprived child is how and when can either society as a whole or through the educational system, change the attitudes and values found in the family unit.

REFERENCES

Cruickshank, William M. (ed.) Psychology of Exceptional Children and Youth, Englewood Cliffs, New Jersey: Prentice-Hall, Inc., 1967.

DeHaan, Robert F. and Havighurst, Robert J., Educating Gifted Children, Chicago: The University of Chicago Press, 1961.

Gallagher, James J., Teaching The Gifted Child, Boston: Allyn and Bacon, Inc., 1964.

Gold, Milton J., Education of the Intellectually Gifted, Columbus, Ohio: Charles E. Merril Books, Inc., 1965.

LEARNING DISABILITIES

Learning disabilities is a term that is compatible with the educational system. Through the years that learning disabilities has become popular, we we have seen a number of different nomenclatures attached to this specific area of disabilities. One will occasionally happen upon terms such as minimal brain dysfunction, specific learning disabilities, perceptually handicapped , perceptually immature, dyslexia, word blindness, hyperkinetic syndrome, hypokinetic syndrome , attention span syndrome, clumsy child syndrome, aphasic, and dysgraphia, all of which are subsidies within the area of learning disabilities.

We cannot say t h a t there is an equation between any of these and the term learning disabilities. The child may be dyslexic but this does not necessarily mean he is a learning disabled child. Also, if the child is categorized as a learning disability child, it doesn't necessarily mean that he possesses all of those particular handicaps.

The learning disabled child may be involved somewhat in reading. He may have behavioral problems. T h e r e are a number of manifestations that could be involved with this child. This particular child about whom we are talking is not a mentally retarded child. He is not a child who has severe hearing problems. He is not a child with severe sight problems. He is not a child who has s e v e r e motor involvement. A severe motor involvement may mean s u c h limits as cerebral palsy may effect in a child. The learning disabled child has average or above average mental ability, but he is probably performing academically below his m e n t a l ability; he may have secondary emotional, social, or c u l t u r a l kinds of problems that may be quite disruptive to the c l a s s - room and at home.

T h e r e are a number of characteristics that are observable by the classroom teacher and by the parent w h i c h may provide some clues a s t o whether or not their child, or children, are involved in learning disability perceptual problem areas. These children will have a tendency t o make r e v e r s a l s on numbers, or letters, such as b's and d's and q's, and p's. They also may have inversions of numbers, for example writing 17 for 71. Some of these children have mir-ror writing. They may write in an upside-down-backward manner, so that if you hold up a mirror you can see perfect writing.

There will be some possible coordination problems. A child may appear somewhat awkward, maybe frequently tripping over his own feet, bumping into things. We should be careful to separate these awkward conditions from the child who may just be the ornery acting-out child without a learning problem. These learning disabled children will have problems in audio-discrimination such as sound-alike words, dime and diamond. Dime/diamond, they would have confusion in sorting out sound-alike words. This situation is not a hearing problem, but it is an inability auditorily to discriminate certain sounds and catagorize the sounds appropriately.

These kids may have a peseveration problem. Perseveration does not mean the same thing as perservering. Perservering is great. This is what a child does on a task if he stays with it until it is completed. The child who perseverates is the child who will do a task, and he will do it; and he will do it again; and he will do it again; and he will do it again. There is no end to the task. Many times he will start a task; erase it, and start over; erase and start over; erase amd start over. He will do two or three lines, erase it and start over; get mad; tear up the paper; break the pencil; and never complete a satisfactory task.

This child may also be hyperactive. A hyperactive child is one who has difficulty in screening out the stimuli that comes to him. You may be sitting in a room while you are reading this article and there may be noise around you such as the shuffling of papers. The door may slam. You can hear the air conditioner or the heater system. Somebody is making noise in the other room, but this isn't distracting to you. You are able to screen out the extra stimuli. These things involve his environment at all times; consequently, it creates a very short attention span. He becomes involved with the task at hand and as he tries sorting through the tasks, he cannot sort out the stimuli that keeps bombarding him. Therefore, you have a child involved in a very serious kind of academic problem. If he is unable to sit at his desk and do the arithmetic, the reading, the writing, or whatever school task is required of him, because of the bombarding stimuli he then becomes something of a problem to himself and to the teacher.

Learning disabled children will sometimes have very poor handwriting, art work, and drawing. The inability to coordinate eye-hand movements are indications that these kids will have trouble performing on group tests of intelligence or achievement. You give a child a group test, 30 kids in a room all taking the same test; before this child is able to achieve on this particular instrument he will have to be able to read, and of course if this child is having reading problems, he will not do well on a group test.

A situation that may be quite noticeable with these kids is in their general performance. In their general environment they will appear brighter than the tests show them to be and we get indications that tell us that this child is not retarded, but there is just something missing; we know that he can do these things if he has the right kinds of opportunities. This feeling is also evident with the child himself. He will have a kind of feeling which says to himself, "Well, I know I can do this. I'm just as smart at the other kids, I know I can do it. But something is wrong and for some reason I can't do it." This is a child who has poor perception of time and space. He may get lost easily. He may not be able to tell time. He gets confused in physical locations and can't understand where he is.

We should use concrete kinds of demands upon these kids, or even singular kinds of demands. For example, "Get out of bed and come to breakfast," rather than, "Get up from bed, put on your shoes and your clothes, and go brush your teeth, and wash your hands, hang the towel up, make your bed, pick up your clothes, come in and eat breakfast." By the time we give the child all these orders he is so busy trying to sort them out, he gets confused, and may well end up unable to do any of them. Sometimes a child may look at you in a very confused kind of manner when you give a long list of orders, because he is having problems trying to sort out all of this information.

Poor perception gives them a problem sometimes in categorizing and associating. For example, you may have four flying objects such as a bird, a helicopter, an airplane, and a kite; then you toss in a car a turtle, and a baseball. Now, if you ask the child to put together the four objects with one thing in common, he may not be able to sort out the four objects that are flying objects. He may toss in a ball or he may toss in the turtle.

These inconsistencies may be tragical in the academic setting. The child may recognize a word today and may not recognize the same word tomorrow. We aren't consistent in our teaching methods and this is a very important aspect to this particular child because he lacks perceptual consistency. He has the inability to perceive an object as having different qualities or varying properties, such as size, position, and shape. He may look at a capitol "A" and a small "a" and these are not recognized as being the same object. He looks at a firetruck from the back, from the front, and from the side, and he is unable to recognize it from all angles as a firetruck. This inability to recognize an object from any view causes subsequent problems when this child goes to school. He is faced with books with different sizes of print, different colored letters, different kinds of type in the letters, and other kinds of varying qualities.

There is also a number of emotional - affective kinds of characteristics that are observable to the teacher and parent with this particular learning disabled child. This is a child who has the ability of affecting; in other words, he kind of overreacts to stimuli. He sometimes has inadequate impulse control. An example of this may be that a child may work for a period of time on a school task, perhaps a picture, a painting, writing assignment, or whatever, and at the end of this task he loses control of himself and becomes quite emotional with crying outbursts and ridicule of himself and others. He simply does not have the ability to control those affective tones that are involved with the completion of the tasks.

This is a child who embellishes the task at hand whether it's reading a story out loud or whether it's telling a story or adding details to pictures. It's something like the perseveration that we spoke of earlier in this article, and it just seems that the child has the inability to stop himself. He may start a story and then keep the story going, going, and going. The suggestions for the teachers and parents at this particular point would be that one should not appear interested and agree with the child's story and continue listening, nor should one reject the child and tell him to shut up, stop adding to the story, and call him a liar. Instead of agreeing or rejecting, one should try to detour him down another avenue of conversation.

These kids will have a very low frustration tolerance. Many times if they don't get immediate success on a task, or they don't get the results they desire immediately, they may react somewhat as one in a paranoid state of affect. They will attack the object or the person who they feel is hindering the situation. As an example, a boy doesn't get the immediate success he wants from drawing a picture. He may attack the picture, rip it up, and break the pencil. He may attack the teacher, because the teacher didn't give him the grade that he needed or wanted on this particular assignment. The emotional procedure of avoiding failure is to attack the failing situation. The teacher may attempt to help a child or correct his papers to show him where he made a mistake, and the child will try to avoid this situation by attacking the teacher with such language as, "You're stupid and the school's stupid and I don't want you to look at my paper."

A child may not respond to any of the demands that the parent makes and this way the parent becomes upset and the child somewhat gets even with his parents. Parents should maintain, or at least try to control this situation simply by being aware of the child's tensions. The parent should be alert to the emotional build up within the child and realize the child may be beginning to reach the end of his toleration point. He can no longer tolerate the task. He can no longer tolerate the teacher or himself. He's about ready to blow a fuse. As parents and teachers, if we can learn to recognize these clues before the explosion, then we would naturally prevent ourselves from having a lot of trouble with the child.

There are a number of suggested kinds of methods and procedures for working with these children in this day and age, but my personal feeling at this time is that we are still in an experimental stage. There is very little evidence of research which indicates static procedures or techniques for the learning disabled child. It was only a few years ago when we believed these children were unable to stand the stimuli in the classroom and we had recommendations to discard bulletin boards, don't put up bright curtains, keep a bland room, and keep toys out of sight, because these kids couldn't tolerate these stimuli. However, I have noticed recently in visiting classrooms and talking with teachers, that these stimuli weren't necessarily disturbing the children. I've been in classrooms which appear to be in total chaos, not because of the bombarding stimuli but as a result of the teacher's inability to tolerate the situation. I've been in other teacher's classrooms which were beautifully decorated. There were all kinds of stimuli existing and the children were performing very well, which indicates to me that the most important factor in this situation was the teacher's ability to maintain the class, rather than how much stimuli was coming from the outside.

I presently believe there are varying success factors in the area of learning disabilities, and my suggestion to parents would be for them to accept that which is most advantageous to them and to their particular child. I think that the main thing we have to realize at this point is that all of the methods and procedures that are indicated for a learning disabled child are not appropriate for all learning disabled children. Some children will need specific kinds of things that will not work work with other children. The same for each child is like saying we all must be aware of and appreciate the same model car; that nobody has a choice. There are also no individual needs to be considered. We realize that this is not the way the world rotates. Some things work for some kids and some things work for other kids. Some methods of raising kids work for some parents and the same methods of raising kids don't work for other parents. So let's not become conclusive; there is no panacea for the learning disabilities child.

REFERENCE

Van Osdol, Wm. R. and Shane, Don G., Exceptional Children, Psychology - Survey, Kendall Hunt, W. C. Brown Publishing Co., Dubuque, Iowa, 1972.

When giving attention to mental retardation we have to speak somewhat in terms that are relative to the child's age, the child's physical and mental maturity, the child's particular environment, and the family needs. Essentially any of us may be retarded if we are placed into a facility for which we are not adequately prepared. It just happens that many of these children are inadequately prepared to meet the demanding pressures that are placed upon them in the public school systems.

To enable the child to utilize completely the public services available to him, we need to categorize mental retardation into groups within the total mentally retarded area. These different groups would be specifically as follows: One group will be an IQ range from approximately "0" to approximately "30-35." This group is referred to as the children who generally need a program which provides total care. These children will probably be involved in some kind of residential setting; that is a state school, a private school, or some other kind of residential setting. These are children who undoubtedly have the inability to care for themselves in many respects. The chances are that many children will not be able to feed themselves adequately, to clothe themselves, to maintain themselves through physical hygiene. In general, they will be the more severely involved kids so far as all self-help skills are concerned. These children probably will not be in a public school situation, because of their inabilities to maintain themselves; consequently, most of these children will be placed

210

by their parents into c a r e centers or residential
centers.

The second group of retarded children is that
group which is educationally referred to as the trainable mentally retarded.   This group of children will
possess IQ's ranging from approximately 30-35 to approximately 50-55.   Trainable has a definition that
is meaningful so far as the public school system is
concerned.   By definition this merely means that the
child is trainable.   He is not a child who will profit from the t r a d i t i o n a l educational program such
as reading, writing, and arithmetic.   He is a child
who can learn a number of skills, self-help skills. He
will be able to learn to feed himself, clothe himself,
and take care of his physical hygiene needs.   Many of
these children will be involved in sheltered workshop
kinds of situations in which they can be adequately
trained for certain jobs.   Probably, though, most of
these children will always need some kind of support.
They will probably not become self-sufficient or self-
determined enough that they can maintain themselves
on a full time job.   They may work in sheltered work-
shops, but they will require additional support from
their parents, communities, and local agencies.

These children will have limited vocabularies.
They can speak and they can carry on a conversation
but it will be of a limited nature.   They will not
be able to c o m m u n i c a t e educationally in terms of
writing, spelling, and arithmetic.   They will probably be able to count numbers, and they can identify
nickels, dimes, and quarters; but if they were asked
to make change for twenty-five cents or to subtract
twenty-five cents from a dollar, this would probably

be almost impossible for them. I think our expectations of these children probably will have a considerable effect upon what progress is witnessed from them. If we feel that they are strictly care patients, and they should be confined to a care agency of some kind; then we will probably not achieve a productive, interested response from these children. Consequently, we do have reasonable kinds of expectations in which these kids can be involved in a sheltered work program, and we let them receive support from those who are concerned; then these children can learn to become as self sufficient as possible, relative to their own disabilities.

The next group of retarded children is that with the largest portion of the population. This group of children is referred to as the educable group; again, "educable" has a definite educational meaning. These are children whose IQ's range from approximately 50-55 on up to 70-75-80. Most states have a cut-off at 78, which is compatible with the federal agency employments such as civil service jobs. This group of kids will have an educational experience that has academic meaning such as reading, writing, and arithmetic. Many of these children can learn to read on a third, fourth, or even fifth grade level. If the child can possibly reach an approximate fourth grade reading level; he will be able to do a number of educational skills. We should realize, though, that before a child is able to achieve the apex of educational learning, he must be exposed to a good teaching situation, a good educational situation, a good home situation, and he must have a self-concept that is not too self-defeating.

Most of these children should eventually be able

to find a place in this world. They will not become engineers at Cape Kennedy, but it is felt that they can find many employment opportunities. Our objectives in education are designed to help these children find personal efficiency, self esteem, self determination, and social efficiency, which may enable him to get along with his peers and maintain a proper social kind of relationship with the world at large. Therefore, it's somewhat reasonable to believe that if a child achieves social and personal efficiency, then chances are that economic efficiency will take care of itself. It is felt that if he has personal and social efficiency, the chances are good that he will be able to find a job, maintain himself on his job, learn the skills of the job, and get along with people, and involve himself in a social way that is acceptable in different forms of employment.

We have a vast number of follow-up studies concerning these educable children in school, in the vocational aspect, in married life, as parents, and as individuals who support themselves and contribute to society in general; it is indeed, conclusively shown that success can be measured by these youngsters. A good example is shown in one area of the United States. A couple of years ago educable students in the high school work-study program, involving about fourteen high schools in the Oklahoma City area, made over $248,000.00 during the school year. These students had many different jobs, rates of pay, and job tenure, but the program definitely proves the point that these young people can become productive citizens in this society.

SECTION FOUR

INFLUENTIAL BEHAVIOR

ABSOLUTES

Parents and teachers, have you _ever_ noticed how much we adults talk in absolute terms to the younger people? "You always, never, are, don't, won't, will, will not, absolutely, positively, without a doubt... the worst kid in town." We seem unable to recognize that the child can perform an adequate task.

For two months the child sits at the dinner table and is a neat, careful little boy. One night he spills his milk. "You _always_ spill your milk. Every time you sit down, you spill your milk. You _can't_ do anything right." What about the two months between spilling; did you ever say? "Johnny really is a neat little boy at the dinner table."

Teachers, as you look around your classroom and you see a student with his hand in the fish bowl, you respond, "Johnny, get your hand out. It will kill the fish. You _absolutely_ know better. I know you know better, but you _always_ do the wrong things." These kinds of reactions cause the kids to wonder, "What's wrong with that stupid, this won't kill the fish. How does she know I _always_ do wrong, I do lots of things right. Boy, what a nut she is."

"Get out of that tree Johnny, you _will_ _fall_ and break your arm." "Gosh that's strange, because I've been climbing trees all my life and I haven't fallen. How come he says I'll break my arm?" Parents, teachers, if you must warn the children, then do so without the absolutes. We don't know for sure that he will break his arm. We may suggest, "Johnny you may fall, but be careful." The child can accept realistic suggestions, but he may not accept an absolute statement, "You are positively going to break your arm."

So many kids are really hurt when parents and teachers fail to see the good that children do, but consistently respond to their children's mistakes, "You never do things the way you should." Really, people, to whom can the child turn if he is subservient to parents and teachers, and he is the one who never does things right. The child will respond, "Shoosh, that teacher is nuts. These things won't happen. How stupid can he be?"

Be aware of your responses to your kids and really discover how many times you can catch yourself saying absolute statements. I think you may enjoy your kids more and I'm quite sure they will enjoy you more.

ADOPTED CHILDREN

I only have one really important point to be indicated to the parents and teachers who are involved with adopted children. This point is to realize a situation in which you are able to defense your own inabilities to be adequate parents, or to defense your inadequacies of being unable to teach children.

Adopted children give parents and teachers the opportunity to allow blame for whatever the child's problem may be upon the fact that he is adopted; and it wasn't our (the adopted parents') fault, but it was someone else's fault that he is the way he is. He was born that way. "His real parents caused his problems before we got him and it's not our fault."

What we are saying is in effect that as parents of an adopted child, as teachers in the classrooms with adopted children, we have a ready-made excuse if the child fails. All we have to do is say, "It's not my fault. It's somebody else's fault. He is adopted you know."

We have observed statistically a couple of facilities in which we have worked with emotionally disturbed children, that from 60 to 80 per cent of the children in these facilities with emotional problems are adopted children. Now, I think, it is extremely important at this point that you don't identify with this situation if you have adopted children within your home. If you are involved in an adopted situation of any kind, don't identify with these percentages because I am not saying that all adopted children will have emotional problems. I am, though, simply saying that if you are living within the framework of an adopted child; then it is important, extremely important, that you become aware of your excuses for your inabilities.

You should not be quick and ready to blame somebody else for your problems of child rearing. I actu-

ally had a couple of parents in my office with a problem child, and this happened to be an adopted child.
While we were discussing the history of the family
situation, the parents were very quick to remind me
that, "We adopted him when he was four months old you
know; therefore, whatever his problems are, they were
surely caused the first four months of life."

Consequently, awareness of self is my only point
when I talk about adopted children. I do not want to
discuss the merits for or against adopting children,
because I think these are all individual family decisions that are quite unique to the individual mothers
and fathers. Adoption is not a situation which can
be generalized, but I do feel quite strongly that you,
as adopted parents, should be aware that you should
not use a ready-made defense (other parents) as an
explanation for whatever your problems may be at home
with your adopted children. If you are having problems at home with your adopted child, then face up
to the fact that probably these problems exist because
of you, not because of the child's previous parents,
and this is especially true when we are talking about
extremely young adopted children.

Now, sure there can be some exceptions to a rule,
but if so these exceptions are probably related more
readily to older adopted children. If you don't get
a child until he is 13, 14, or 15, naturally there has
to be considerable attention given to the fact that
he was quite a bit older when you adopted him. Even
so, parents, it should not be a total excuse for you
and the child's inabilities to live with, work with,
and adapt to the family scene.

I'm not going to discuss the reasons why you

have adopted children, or why you may want to adopt children, or the reasons within your own families for adopting one, two, three, or more children. Our concern is that you don't use the child as a scape goat; don't blame the adopted child for the problems within your home situation.

ATTENTION--ACCEPTANCE

There is one thing common among most people and it is also extremely common among children, and that is the equation of attention with acceptance. What the child is saying is, "If I can get attention, that means that I am accepted." Consequently, he will express himself in many different ways to get the attention that he needs so much. The child in the classroom, who asks the teacher a question and is somewhat ignored with a casual comment and by-passed, is seeking attention. He is seeking attention really in a rather positive kind of way, but it is obvious that if he doesn't get attention in an acceptable manner; he will command attention in a negative way; which would probably be by acting out and causing trouble. He, then, through poor behavior gets the attention he desires from the parents or teacher; which to him means, that he has been accepted.

Many times it is the fault of the parents and teachers that a child has to resort to the negative way of getting this greatly needed attention. An example of this would be as follows: A child is striving t o get attention from his parents o r h i s teacher in some acceptable way. As I have just mentioned, the child's good attempts are ignored, ignored, and ignored; finally he expresses himself in such a deviate way that his behavior cannot be ignored, and attention is given to him. The resulting attention though is u s u a l 1 y punishment or discipline, but he has commanded the adults attention. I think a good rule w o u 1 d b e for parents and teachers w h o have children wanting recognition f o r some little job or well-done task is to give the children positive support. When children ask questions or make comments, we should respond to them in ways that are meaningful to the children's questions rather than ignoring them.

We probably even extend this kind of concept into racial relationships . M a n y times minority groups may strive to get attention, and by getting attention this means that they are accepted. They may try very, very positive ways and a r e ignored. S o finally a riot i s started and all kinds of attention is given to them. W e have to attend to tragedies, i t can't be avoided. We do the same thing at home and in our classrooms. We wait until a n e a r riot erupts before we attend to the task at hand.

Parents and teachers should give that child an opportunity t o express himself and make comments on things that are at least relative to his world. Don't stifle when he is trying to d o something in a positive, normal kind of way. Help h i m over the obstacles by attending to good behavior. If the child is attended for good performance, I believe y o u will avoid many situations that would cause him to deviate in his behavior.

AFFECT --INTELLECT

Affect and intellect are probably two of the most significant processes relative t o one's behavior . One problem that exists is that so many people do not understand the conscious and unconscious motivations of behavior. Motivation is the factor that controls one's behavior--the affective tones, t h e feeling tones--the things that may be unconscious within our relative framework. Yet, this unconscious motivation may dictate to us to do whatever it is we are doing; even though we may con sciously and intellectually know that we are emitting poor behavior.

An example would be that one may know intellectually t h a t he should n o t run a red light or stop sign. He k n o w s this is not right; he knows it is wrong. It could cause an accident; y e t, one day he pulls up to a corner; he doesn't hesitate; he goes on. After he has run the stop sign, then he thinks back, "Why did I do that?" Then he gives himself a reason for having done what he did. Intellectually h e has a reason. Affectively he does not k n o w why he ran through the stop sign.

Okay, there's a lot of behavior in children and people that is caused by the affective level of motivation, the emotional overtone in one's life. Affec—

tivity is a very behaviorally controlling f a c t o r. Therefore, a parent who screams and yells at the child, "You k n o w better. You knew better. W h y d i d you do it?" and then expects the child to give a g o o d answer for his behavior is not a parent wh o realized the potential of a child's lack of affective control.

Another example is that the child has misbehaved in some way. He did something of which you the parent or teacher do not approve. S o immediately you rush to the child and you start questioning him, "Why did you do that? Why did you do that? Now y o u tell me why you did that?" So the child responds. He gives you an answer. His answer doesn't seem appropriate to you and you respond, "You k n o w t h a t's not right. That's not a good answer. Now, you tell me the truth. You tell me why you did that." The child still can't answer He doesn't know why he did it. It happened . He can't explain why he did it. C a n y o u, mother, father, teacher, tell me why you d o everything that you do? Can you tell m e w h y you may s i t and pick at your fingernails, chew your pencil, tap your finger on the desk, wiggle your leg? Can you describ e and evaluate all of those little idiosyncratic kinds of behavior to which you can attach no significance, yet you are doing them? Can you tell m e why? Y o u really can't explain your behavior a n y better than the child can tell you why h e may throw a piece o f paper at the child across the classroom from him. He can't tell you why he did it, but he did it, and he intellectually knows he did it.

There seems t o b e a n equilibrium process that exists within all of us as we strive f o r balance in our world. But the obstacle is that many times we don't know what it is we're trying to balance. Consequently our behavior goes into a rather irrational kind of path. After we have traveled this path to uncertainty we then look back intellectually and try figuring out why we did that which we did. Well, the intellectual defense is needed. There is no question that one needs defense mechanisms in life. If we do something wrong we need to be able to defend ourselves, and make an excuse for what we did; rationalize our behavior and give ourselves reasons. We would be extremely uncomfortable people if we were unable to defend our behavior.

The main point of this conversation is to help teachers and parents to be aware of the fact that kids do not necessarily have total control over their actions and reactions at all times. Many times these kids are just as disturbed at themselves for what they have done wrong as we the adults are, and many times these kids would dearly love to do better. But for some unconscious reason they aren't able to control affectively and emotionally their behavior, and they really don't know why. Consequently, they become victims of their own inabilities to handle their situations. And we as adults hop on top of them and pound them down a little more by cramming it down, telling them, "You knew better than that. Why did you do it?"

Again, teachers and parents, I am not saying that we should be complacent and let the child live with poor behavior. What I am saying is that we should not pile undue kinds of blame and pressures on a child for behavior over which he has no control, and for behavior which he too wishes were different, and for

h i s undesirable actions w h i c h h e hopes one d a y
to master.

ABILITY—LEVEL OF ASPIRATION

When you, parents and teachers, say to your kids,
"I know you can do better." You probably in fact do
not know that he can do better. Achievement and ability become circular. One does not know ability until
one produces. After the child has achieved, then we
can say he has the ability, but we cannot say he has
the ability before he achieves. "He has the ability,
but he just does not apply himself." I f h e cannot
apply himself, we must assume that h e doesn't have
the ability. Ability is achievement. Achievement
is ability.

Our teacher and p a r e n t aspirations may sound
great to us, but to the non-aspiring child we remain
incompatible. We must examine o u r expectations and
aspirations quite realistically. I am not suggesting
that we should be void of, or have static e xpecta-
tions; but we must have aspirations that are compatible with the rate of growth of the child. We should
be careful not to confuse aspirations with abilities,
because we may not know where the child's a bili t y
stops, and where parent aspirations begin.

When we really become intent upon discover i n g

an aspiration level that is compatible for the child we must first consider the individual c h i l d . We should work through his maintenance of himself, and not place him into a competitive, defeating environment with 50 other children. Degrees of success can mean many things to different children.

Our parental and teacher aspirations should not be for the whole domestic or school milieu, but instead we should indicate separate realistic aspirations for each individual child. We shall probably always remain different from each other and that which is good for one m a y b e d i s a s t e r f o r another. We no longer say, "All the other kids a r e able to, why aren't you?" Each child is different. Each of the parent's and teacher's aspiration levels for that child is different. Therefore, we may destroy individual children by placing them into expected environments which far exceed their levels of functioning. Each child's level of expectation can be discovered, developed, and polished i f we as teachers and parents will stop instilling our unrealistic demands for achievement upon the child. Again, I say, "Don't become complacent, b u t please b e realistic when you try equating your level o f aspiration to the child's level of aspiration."

BODY INFLUENCES OF BEHAVIOR

One's body image may have a very positive or negative influence upon one's behavior. There is considerable evidence that indicates that the influence of behavior relative to one's image of self is quite significant. The actual influence the body has upon a child's behavior is extremely difficult for parents to determine. The body image does, without a doubt, though, have an influence over one's behavior.

When I refer to body influences I am not necessarily regulating that which is representative of something abnormal in size, of shape, or a deformity, or a lack of muscle and body proportions. To determine how much influence the body has upon oneself is not in direct proportion to the adequacy or size of the physical body itself, but upon the person's body image of himself. That is to say that young boys or girls may have very fine body proportions, good shape and physical appearances; but they may view themselves as something terrible or as something other than what is physically actual.

A person may reflect images upon himself, that are not true images if he has a poor image feedback from mother, father, or teacher. Some examples would be situations in which a parent or teacher may constantly refer to a child's lazy body, his stupid slump; his inability to walk straight; to keep his shoulders erect; to hold his tummy in, etc. Eventually the child may begin to view himself as one who

227

possesses these qualities of abnormal body character which actually do not exist.

It is also very difficult to determine whether the projected self image influences behavior, or whether the behavior influences the poor self image that one has of himself. I think the most important aspect concerning this particular situation, is for parent and teacher to be aware that they can feed back to a child many negative kinds of concepts of himself. And as parents and teachers we need to be extremely careful that we don't directly, indirectly, or subtly pronounce a child to be something other than what he is. We need to recognize the assets of the child and not refer to the child by saying, "You are always sloppy, your hair is never combed, your clothes are dirty, your face is dirty, your teeth need brushing, your ears are dirty, and you need to take a bath." Parents and teachers, can't we project just a few of the good things about these kids each day? You may be surprised by the change in the child's behavior if he receives a few good words.

Poor body image and body influence on behavior is evident through the many examples that have appeared from the hollywood scene. The movie star is projected to the public as a beautiful, physical, intelligent person; but the person himself, the movie star, doesn't realize these same feedbacks. He looks upon himself as something worse than his public image. He unconsciously sees himself as nondeserving of the attention that he is getting and as a result the final goal of a star may be to terminate his image by suicide or through self-destruction with alcohol and drugs.

Therefore, parents, be aware that your child can be mentally healthy, whether his body is six feet tall and weighs 170; or whether h e i s five feet two and weighs 130. It is still a matter o f accepting and living with, and realizing that which is within one's own body resources, rather than the projected expectancies of some channelized public. How the c h i l d lives his real life situations is how the child feels about himself, which may not reflect how he physically appears to the public. Remember, though, his image can change if he receives consistent negative or positive reinforcement.

I do realize that our society projects a considerable amount of attention upon the perfect physical being, the beautiful person. This body attention is generated a little more each year in the form of movies, television, sports, beauty contests, magazine ads, best dressed man and woman, big man o n campus a n d numerous o t h e r competitive situations. We must, though, help our children to realize that we see beauty and resources within individuals, not solely because they are physically beautiful and walk without a limp, but because they respond t o themselves and t o the people around them as worthy components of their lives.

BROKEN HOMES -- DIVORCE -- WORKING MOTHERS

There seems to be some kind of an evil associa-

tion with divorce and its relationship to the adjustment of children from these broken homes. Surely, we
can find raw statistics which indicate a large number
of maladjusted children come from broken homes, but
there may not be evidence to support the fact that a
broken home caused the disorder. This child may have
had problems regardless of a divorced home.

I believe there are many situations which justify the separations of mother and father for the kid's
benefit. How many times have you heard? "We've got
to stay together for the benefit of the children."
That reasoning is totally ridiculous. There is no
basis for staying together because of the children.
Many of these kids would be far more comfortable living with one solid parental identification, rather
than in a state of ambivalence with both parents. The
child needs, badly, someone upon whom he can rely
for strength, structure, and decision. Consequently,
he is more likely to receive this structure and support from one good parent than he is from the two
fighting parents who constantly place the child as an
object of attention between their quarrels and fights.

In almost all broken homes the mother will have
the responsibility to raise the children, which, granted, is a mammoth task. Child development can be accomplished by the mother, and she quite likely will
do a better job than the father could have done. Of
course, mother, you will not be able to meet your
children's needs and function successfully if you constantly tell yourself, "The kids need a father, I don't
know what I'm going to do. I can't handle these kids
by myself. Oh, why did this have to happen?" Okay,

it happened and you can arrive at your destination of good motherhood by giving the children an image of strength. Don't involve the children in a hate campaign against dad. Don't involve them in all the whys and why nots of your marriage failure. These kids will not grow emotionally strong and secure if they are faced with the ambivalence of hating and loving their mother and father. Even if you justifiably hate your ex-husband, don't burden the kids with these open attacks upon him. This teaches them to hate also. You will serve as a model for your children. The kids need warmth and affection, and they need to learn how to love.

Don't use the broken home as an excuse to fail with your children. If your children assume behavioral problems, face yourself and do not blame someone else. Sure, the broken home may produce contributing factors, but in all probability it is not the only cause; instead it may serve as an easy excuse for one's problem children.

One of your greatest concerns, mother, should be the provisions which you make relative to the children's supervision when you are not at home. If you work and arrive home from work at 5:30 pm; be sure to provide care for your child when he gets home alone from school at 3:30 pm. A two hour babysitting fee may pay far more in dividends than one could ever save if your child were to encounter one singular day of severe trauma. Even if a child comes home from school and he's physically, chronologically, and emotionally able to be alone around the house, but he cuts himself severely, breaks an arm, or has in general some kind of an accident, to whom does he turn? He is without support. He is lonely. He hates everybody for his pain and suffering. Even though you may only be a phone call away, he still needs the structure and adult comfort of having someone near in time of needs. Now, I don't mean that one should smother these children, but you should provide for their comfort and safety, if you cannot do so yourself. The same incident as described above could easily happen if mom and dad were living together and were both on jobs and the children were home alone.

The children may need care and provisions if they are living with one or with both parents. Therefore, don't use divorce as your reason to ruin your children. Assume your parental responsibilities without complacency and defense mechanisms that say, "Divorce ruined my life, now my children are being ruined." Many kids have made good lives without either a mother or father; therefore beware, parents, your excuses may only contribute to the discomforts of your children.

CORPORAL—PHYSICAL PUNISHMENT

It is rather difficult for one to defend thoroughly the advantages or disadvantages of corporal punishment, because it is quite evident that there are many situations in which corporal punishment-- physical punishment does work with children. I am also sure that all of us can cite examples in which we have seen children who have been physically and literally beaten to death, and there seems to be no lesson learned. I know you can pick up your newspapers and read "Dear Abby" and "Ann Landers" and a few other columns and you usually receive a very negative picture of physical punishment, that is, the old fashioned kind of spanking or whatever you wish to call the placing of the paddle on the rump of a child.

The fact does remain, though, that there are some children for whom a physical form of punishment is effective, and there are children for whom physical punishment is not effective. I think the key to corporal punishment lies essentially in one area, and that is whether affective tones (A F F E C T) exist between father and son or mother and son or teacher and student. If there is a feeling of affective relationship between child and adult, I think we are free in our assumptions to express totally to the child that this punishment does not represent a bad self-image view, but it does represent a bad situation that the child was in. Consequently, we are not punishing the child because he was a bad child, but we are punishing the child because he in effect, did something wrong.

If these affective tones exist between adult and child then the child is going to get the message that we are punishing him physically because he committed some kind of wrongful act, and we're not punishing him because we don't like him, we can't stand him, he's a nasty, dirty kind of kid. If affective tones do not exist between adult and child, probably whatever form of punishment, physical or other kind, that is administered to a child would not be acceptable for the child. This child is going to resist any opportunity that

233

condemns him as a bad child. He probably already has a good feedback that says, "I am being paddled because I am bad, totally bad. I am no good, I am a bum kid." Therefore, it appears evident that any kind of punishment awarded to this child probably will not be an acceptable form of punishment. You can beat the hell out of him and it won't work; you could talk logic with him, you could plead with him, you could beg with him; but chances are he's going to resist all forms of punishment.

On the other hand, you're going to have the child who has a good affective relationship between himself and an adult and he will be able to accept the fact, "I did something wrong, I'm still a good kid, I'm not totally bad, but I made a mistake; now I must suffer somewhat the limits for making this mistake." He will accept his paddling. He will accept a bawling out. He will accept a stern look, he will accept anything that you give him as a means of saying, "Don't do this again."

Essentially then, what I am saying is, if we have good affective tones existing between adult and child, the chances are excellent that nearly any form of punishment will be acceptable. But if these affective tones do not exist, then probably no form of punishment will really be affective for this child. In fact, punishment to this child may be a rewarding situation. This child may not get any attention from adults except that which is in the form of punishment; therefore, he is content to do something wrong to get the hell beat out of him, which means he is getting attention, some way, somehow, from the adult world. I'm not saying that it is good attention, but I am saying it is attention, and that's the thing the child seeks. What he is doing is getting some-thing rather than nothing, and if he has to have himself physically punished to achieve an attentive goal, then that he will do.

My goal is not for or against physical punish-ment. It is quite clear that I am saying, "Corporal punishment is neither good nor bad, but it is an ef-fective situation for some children. It is very non-effective with other children, and I think as parents and teachers we must thoroughly examine the situation within our own homes and schools and classrooms, to determine what child can be accepting of physical punishment and what child cannot be accepting of this kind of punishment."

If we are able to discriminate accurately, then we should be able to administer that which is physical-ly compatible to a child and that which is not phys-ically compatible. A child with a good relationship between adults and himself will probably be a child who would respond to any kind of punishing terms ; and we therefore, can very easily cast out different theories that say totally, unequivocally, and absolute-ly, that physical punishment should never be used. Really, people, what it amounts to is, if it works, use it. If it doesn't work, find something else.

CAUSE FOR BEHAVIOR

As parents and teachers we many times make very foolish statements relative to behavior. We have a way of passing off all kinds of excuses for a child's behavior such as: "He was born that way. His parents don't care. The kid is no damn good, and he is a bum, and he never will be any good, and he has bad genes, bad blood, poor protoplasm or whatever." Anyhow, I think we really need to realize that whatever behavior exists within the repertoire of the child, that the emission of this behavior is caused by something or by other people. A child just doesn't manifest behavior; there's a reason for what he is doing, and any time we have a child emitting certain kinds of unpopular, unfitting behavior, I think that we should realize that there is probably a reason for this behavior.

It just doesn't happen that he has learned to perform the way he performs unless he has had a model to follow or some kind of traumatic kinds of experiences during a certain time in his life that have reflected upon his behavior. The fact remains, though, that there is at least some sort of an ideology connected with a child's behavior.

I think many times we find these pseudo kinds of concepts relative to behavior manifestations in order to excuse our own inabilities to handle the situation at hand. An example would be that the child is misbehaving in some way in the classroom, or at home, and the parent or teacher excuses his behavior because he was born that way or by some other ridiculous kind of statement which, in effect is saying, "I have an excuse for not being able to handle the child's behavior." It's a way of saying, "This child has problems, and I didn't cause the problems. I don't need to know how to handle the problems, because they are inexcusable and there would be no point in trying

to work w i t h the child because he will never change
anyhow."

I think i f we can just somewhat understand that
t h e r e is a cause f o r the child's behavior, then at
lease w e should be able to work with the children on
a m o r e empathetic kind of approach. Consequently,
we wouldn't become critical, demanding, and pressuring
of the child; we would though, have some understanding
that the child really has problems.

He probably doesn't r e a l l y enjoy behaving the
way he behaves either, b u t t h e r e is probably something within him that's commanding h i m to do many of
the unfit, undesirable activities. S o the next time
you have a problem with a child, try not excusing your
inabilities to w o r k with him b y saying that he has
some strange etiology f o r his behavior and you can't
help the cause or the symptom.

CHEATING

Cheating is a situation which i s very threatening to teachers and parents,but I venture to say t h a t
nearly all cheating situations are constituted through
t h e unreasonable demands on children by parents and
teachers. I believe i n the basic concept of honesty
relative to the superego or conscience of t h e child.
Kids learn to be honest; kids l e a r n not to c h e a t.
Kids learn to gravitate to the expectations of teachers and parents, and many times if these expectations

are of a negative consequence, the child will fulfill the role expected of him.

Example, if we expect the students to be dishonest, they may very well be dishonest. I was teaching a group of high school mentally retarded students a few years ago, and in this class the students were always wanting to borrow money. They would need a nickel or dime for a variety of reasons. Finally, one day I told the class that each of us would put twenty cents in a jar and use it as a bank. If a student needed to borrow money, he would write his name and the amount borrowed on a piece of paper, take the money and leave the paper in the jar. When he repaid the loan he would take out the paper with his name and amount, or change the amount if he only repaid part of his loan. This money jar was left on my desk, day and night. I never lectured the students about stealing and honesty. I expected them to be honest and did not indicate any concern about stealing. Our jar was empty many times, but the kids always payed their debts, and we did not lose any money. In fact, that jar sat on my desk all year and we never had anyone steal from it.

What are your expectations, teachers and parents? Do you constantly caution your kids about cheating or stealing? We can make cheats of any students if we make our expectations too unbearable. A professor could make any college class he teaches a group of cheaters by being so unrealistic in his demands that the students could pass only by resorting to all kinds of cheating. He then could set up his testing days in such a routine way that he could catch a few students cheating and in turn prove his point, consciously or unconsciously, that the students couldn't be trusted. "See, I just c a u g h t them, look at the example of our irresponsive young people."   A r e w e to prove how tough we are as teachers and p a r en t s, and that youth can't be trusted, or are we to assume a basic policy of h o n e s t y and let kids learn i n a pleasant, trusting kind of milieu?

If your s t u d e n t s cheat, teachers and parents, you s h o u l d take a long close look a t your demands upon and expectations of these kids. Are you expecting Ph.D. work from a college freshman, or B.A. con c ep t s f r o m young public school children? Be realistic by using some common sense kinds of judgement.

I do consulting work for a private school, Wagon Wheel School, McLoud , Oklahoma, for emotionally dis-turbed children; and this school has a concept of ap-plication which says t h a t l e a r n i n g is a v e r y emotional process, and that the children a r e d o i n g the best they can at any given time. An example would be that if a child causes trouble in school, it is as-sumed that he was, even though disturbing, doing t h e best he could. This i s not a suggestion to b e c o m e complacent, but a suggestion which says, "Help t h e child help himself." The child may not h a v e enough resources to help himself. Therefore, you, the par ent and teacher will need to guide him, not ridicule or punish him for what he may not be able to control.

Cheating will be an isolated situation if y o u will not accuse or demand equality from all students. Sure, you will have occasions of kids cheating, but it will be seldom if you will give the children the opportun-ity to be honest. I'm concerned about the 95%+ number of youngsters who will not cheat. Sure, we will have

the exceptional situation--character disorder, socio-
pathic kind of example, but most of the c h i l d r e n
will be honest if permitted to be so.

Some teachers will pass out test papers to their
students in rotated s e a t order or by different test
forms. W h a t is the immediate feedback o r mess**a**ge
to the student? Why, v e r y simply we a r e saying to
them, "See, I don't trust you. I alternated your test
forms so you cheaters can't cheat." Now, h o w c a n
this really m a k e a student feel trusted, respected,
give self-value and honesty?

I've seen kids say, "My dad's called me a thief
since I was ten years old, so after he called me one for
five years, I m i g h t j u s t as w e l l be one." Yes,
ADULTS, we pressure a n d accuse t h e youngsters into
many patterns of cheating behavior. I firmly believe
t h a t if we express expectations and/o r aspirations
o f honesty toward o u r children we will i n turn receive honesty a n d respect from most o f them. Don't
make the children turn t o cheating or dishonesty because of your unrealistic demands upon them.

CONSCIENCE-SUPEREGO

This will b e a short conversation on conscience
a n d superego, which I believe is an extremely important part of p a r e n t s' and teachers' lives. If you
are involved in t h e early years of teaching or raising children, then y o u must realize that a child may

not know r i g h t from wrong and he may not be able to
r e s p o n d accordingly.   If a c h i l d commits a wrong
task or behaves badly--steals, lies, cheats, whatever;
he does not automatically have a conscience as a r e -
sult of this behavior.

Now the thing that is of great importance during
this period of l i f e is that many children have n o t
reached a level o f conscience development yet.   This
is a period in life when the child should become aware
of r i g h t and wrong and develop a conscience.   This
period m a y be called the period f o r the development
of a superego.   T h i s is a stage of development that
usually b e c o m e s prominent at age four to six for a
child. At this age the child may go to his neighbor's
yard, t a k e a tricycle from the yard next door, come
back home and say, "L o o k what I found n e x t door."
Okay, t h i s is a child who hasn't really learned the
rights and wrongs; to h i m he i s n't stealing.   He
doesn't h a v e the conscience that says he has stolen
a boy's tricycle--that h e is a thief.   Granted, many
t i m e s parents w i l l make a thief out of this child
by walking o u t in the yard yelling, "Y o u dirty little crook, y o u h a v e stolen a tricycle.   It doesn't
belong to you.   Now, you get back over there and give
it back to them, right now, before I blister you good."

T h i s labeling, pressuring, constant bickering
to the child about being a thief may very well be the
precipitating factor that causes h i m to start stealing.   He may rationalize, "If I'm going to b e called
a thief; I may as well be a thief."

Parents and t e a c h e r s , I'm not saying that we
should become complacent and ignore the child's behavior.   Sure we should be constantly teaching the child

the rights and wrongs of l i f e , and letting him know
that there a r e some things we can and cannot do, and
l e t him learn limitations of behavior; but we should
not pressure the fanatics of the r i g h t s and wrongs
to the point t h a t the child will deviate to the opposite of the goal that we have set for him.

This type of behavior may be something that creates a problem during the teacher's day. There could
be c h i l d r e n who are slow to develop a superego or
conscience. Consequently, these kids c a n be in t h e
first, second, or t h i r d grade, and yet not know the
real rights and wrongs of life. There may be the kid
in the classroom w h o i s taking pencils and stealing
lunch money and committing other kinds of deviations,
but the teacher m u s t approach the problem through a
learning procedure t o help the c h i l d realize right
from wrong. We should not approach h i m with a criminal kind of label that ways, "Y o u , kid, are no damn
good, and you are a thief, and I don't trust you anymore." Therefore, parents and teachers, be ca r e f u l
before you start accusing y o u r child, before you
start calling him a thief, liar, and a cheat; because
this child may n o t really know the rights and wrongs
about which you are accusing him. H e may then quite
easily gravitate to the model that the adult has presented, "You are a thief," and he becomes that whic h
he is labeled--a thief.

Inconsistency probably is the most destructive factor leading to emotional disturbance in children. This child who never knows where he stands with mom and dad, and teachers, or what his feelings are toward adults is a very uncomfortable and disorganized child.

Parents and teachers so many times make demands upon their children one day and release them from the consequences another day. If a child really, consistently knows what kind of behavior is expected of him; most of the time, he will gravitate to those values. We adults get caught in the midst of our own guilt feelings and feel that we've been too hard on a child and then give in to him. On Monday we say it is okay to go shopping with another peer. On Tuesday we say it is not proper to be with this certain peer. Wednesday, we give the child a dollar to have fun. Thursday, we tell the child he is spending too much money. With our own values changing inconsistently each day, there is no way the child can regulate his worth. He feels accepted one day, rejected another day, and on the fence another day.

If a child walks into his home each day and is greeted consistently with meaningful words of confidence and acceptance, he'll get the message that parents are pretty good people. If he is greeted consistently each day with a rap on the head and words of distrust, fear, anger, etc., he'll get the message that parents are no damn good. Either of these situations would probably be better than the child who is on the fence trying to decide whether parents are good or bad guys. The accepted, loving parent will get good response and gravitation of the child's values; therefore, t h e child can affectively say t h a t he l o v e s his parents, and really mean what he says. The child who receives consistently bad treatment can honestly call his parents a no good bunch of blankety-blanks and he will not have to bear the conscience of not honoring mother and father; because he has pro of that they are no g o o d , regardless of w h a t society says about honoring father and mother. He knows where he stands. He knows his parents are bad.

The child who has to vacillate between l o v i n g and hating his parents w i l l be a very uncomfortable child. One day he may feel that h e loves father and the next day he wants to kill him. He recognizes that dad was nice to h i m yesterday; therefore, dad isn't such a bad guy. Today dad abuses the boy. Now, where does this youngster stand. He i s confused, hostile, anxious, and possesses doubts of h i s own self-worth.

Consistency is the day. If a parent i s consistently good or consistently b a d, t h e child at least knows h i s limits, but I should hope that all of us-- parents and teachers--may be able to look at o u r relationship w i t h kids and discover how consistent or inconsistent we r e a l l y are. When your consistency to c h i l d growth relative to p a r e n t s and teachers breaks down, you will find yourself with a very manipulative and cleverly objective child. His s u b j e c - tivity disappears a n d he becomes an object of parent manipulation, a n d he becomes a child who can in turn manipulate t h e parent. T h e really tragic aspect of this situation is that the parents usually become the slaves to the child, and the child gravitates to values that can only cause more domestic problems within in the home. Consequently, parents lose t h e respect and values of life from their children, a n d it is clearly and precisely the parents' fault.

DISPLACED AGGRESSION

When y o u see a child at home or school suddenly hit a desk, chair, wall, or another object, h o w do you as a parent and/or teacher respond? "Stop that, we do not hit things. We must be nice and not lose our tempers." Is that a typical response? We so often inhibit out children's feelings. We m u s t always tell the children to contain themselves, then they finally really blow a fuse. Don't you feel good after letting it all out on the golf c o u r s e, at a football game , a night out, dinner, dancing, movies, by fishing. . . We need to be a b l e to express our uptight feelings. We need t o hit a pillow, kick that tree, let out our emotions.

A few years ago at the Wagon Wheel School, McLoud Oklahoma, some boys literally rode an old horse until she fell and died. They then approached the director of the school relative to a science class kind of dissecting project. T h e director somewhat reluctantly said okay. T h i s project turned into a nightmare of cutting and hacking, jumping upon, pulling, a n d severing different parts of the horse's anatomy. At times it seemed as though these k i d s (remember these a r e disturbed kids) were at a frenzied state of destruction. This was aggression. T o w a r d whom w e don't know, but as the chief psychiatrist told us a t staffing, "It's b e t t e r that they destroyed t h e horse, rather than a staff member." Okay, this is an extreme, but my message should b e well conceived that by displacing o u r aggression, we may s a v e ourselves from committing a physical act upon another person.

Another extreme example o f displaced aggression is a sixteen y e a r old boy who lived with his mother who prostituted h e r s e l f and also had had relations with this boy; her own son. This boy would very method-ically build a gallows, rope, and all; and then catch cats and hang them. Yes, it is a terrible picture of destruction, but I'm sure the cat was s y m b o l i c of his prostituting mother and he was killing his mother. It is still better that the boy hung cats rather than attacking his mother. By displacing t h e aggression t o the animals we were able to work with him and get him back into society. Had he really killed his moth-er he would never have had the opportunity t o return to society.

Now, don't get the wrong picture. I'm not saying turn your kid loose a n d let him destroy al l that is around him, but I am saying that there are times when our aggressive tendencies m a y w e l l be displaced on a tree, door, pillow, etc., a n d we w i l l be able to relieve ourselves of some of the tensions. There are l i m i t s for your children at home and school, and I realize that w e can allow kids to express themselves a little more extremely i n a private school, because we have t h e staff to control the situation. Just do not become overly concerned about a child who relieves himself of his frustrations, unless it is a constant, frequent, l o n g tenured behavior, then you may n e e d the help of a counseling agency. The child who kicks a chair, or hits his pillow may be displacing his ag-gression, but at least he is n o t destructive to him-self or other people around h i m. Therefore, parents don't be too quick to discipline these kinds o f displaced feelings. After all, haven't you ever felt like kicking the old car, because it didn't perform adequately?

DRESS--LONG HAIR

The manner of dressing and the grooming of one's hair appears to be a very significant problem in many homes today. Apparently there is a need for the kids to identify with their peers through dress and grooming habits, and there also appears to be a tendency by the parents to identify certain dress and grooming habits with delinquent behavior. I feel that there is a certainty of truth for both the kids and the parents. The kids do need to identify with their peers, and the parents rightfully and logically have associated many behavior deviations with the kids' appearances.

The equation of delinquency and appearance should not sustain a certain kind of clothing or hair length. The equation seems more apparent in the way the young person presents an image of himself. Quite likely a parent may see a young person who has long hair and extremely mod clothing, but is a very neat well-appearing person. The parent may also see a young person with the same hair style and clothing, but this one appears ragged, dirty, and unkept. Therefore, it should be obvious that the deviation comes from within the person's self-image, rather than from the clothing style. A parent may also see another adult who is wearing a suit and tie and he looks very neat, but another adult may be wearing a suit and tie, but he looks the same as the grubby kid appears in his mod clothes.

One does not have to have the latest styles and the most expensive clothes to look well dressed. Cleanliness is a very inexpensive procedure. I do firmly believe,though, that there is a very direct relationship between the way the child presents himself through physical hygiene and his emotional stability. Therefore, parents, if your child is really bugging you through his manner of dress , then maybe you should search further and find out if you have a reason for being upset. I would firmly agree, though, that if your child manifests behavior that is representative of a physically unkept, dirty kid; then I would immediately and consistently redress, clean, and cut the kid's hair . He will undoubtedly resist, he may raise hell, but if he realizes that you mean business and that you are consistent in your demands; he will gravitate to a different and better standard. He will not change for the better, though, if you express a feeling of guilt because you have mistreated him. He will only become more manipulative because he knows that he will win and parents will give in.

Today's contemporary world is more tolerant of extreme styles, but the interesting thing is that any style can look presentable and acceptable if the person manages his appearance. The decision that parents must make relative to clothing and hair styles should be determined by the youngster's ability to wear the styles in an acceptable manner.

248

EMPATHY vs. SYMPATHY

Empathy is a means of expressing emotion that is extremely important when working with exceptional children. It is also extremely important when working with all children. Empathy is a way of expressing or experiencing the same kinds of feelings that are within the emotional framework of another person. One should somewhat be able to feel the same emotions that are expressed by another person. One should be able to understand that a little child feels sadly, and then be able to express a feeling of sadness with the child, not a feeling of sorrow for the child.

Empathy should not be confused with sympathy. Sympathy is expressing a feeling of sorrow for the child. Empathy is expressing a feeling of understanding. The child doesn't need sorrow. It isn't uncommon to hear children at school make comments such as, "The only reason the teacher is doing that is because she feels sorry for me. She doesn't really care anything for me. She just feels sorry for me. She doesn't really like me."

There is no way that you can fool or mislead the children through your expressed feelings. They get the feedback from your expression, the tone of your voice, the impression of your eyes and face. Even an old dumb dog can tell when we like or dislike him, and he doesn't speak or talk to us. He does, though, get a feedback from us that gives him the message. "I like you, dog," or, "I can't stand dogs." Now, really, we will not have contact with children who are less able than some dumb animal to read our feelings; therefore, one of the most tragic things we can say to any child is, "I feel sorry for you. I just don't know what to say or do for you." The child already is reading how you feel about him. You don't have to magnify your feelings then verbally abuse him with sympathetic or pitying words.

What one is really saying when he expresses sympathy for another person is that,"I'm glad it is you, not I. I'm glad that it is you, who is crippled, not I. I'm glad that it is you, who is retarded, not I. I'm glad that it is you, who is disturbed, not I." These feelings are fed back to the underpriviledged person and all other children.

The adult expresses a feeling of superiority, a feeling which is conditioned and says, "I can't accept and like you unless you are able to be a perfect child and come up to my standards and expectations." It isn't enough to say to the child, "You must walk. You must talk. You must go to school." Instead, we say, "You must walk without a limp. You must speak perfectly. You must go to school and make all A's. You cannot be an exception to this rule." If this child doesn't reach these unrealistic adult expectations of growth; we fail to recognize the true feelings that may be present, and then we express our sorrow for this child and his inabilities to cope with school and life, which again emphasizes our sympathy for him as a failure and a no-good kid. Therefore, we must realize within ourselves that we need to express a feeling of understanding and an awareness of the child's emotions, and then avoid saying, "I am sorry for you."

The total effects of environmental influence on behavior is a very difficult task to determine. We have to assume though that there are influences within the environments in which people live. The amount of food one has to eat; the kind of job that one has; the kind of clothes that one wears; the involvements with legal authorities; the care and attention within the home from mother and father; and the actual rights and wrongs of social living; all, have an influence on one's behavior. A child will branch out from his little world only if he has the experience or opportunity to grow. If he has not had contact with associative, categorization, and conceptionalization models through experiential frameworks, his behavior will be very limited to a certain milieu of life.

To be adequate in this world we must be able to perform in a number of roles. If a child lives in a stagnant environment, then that environment is going to influence his ability to perform the various roles that are required of him. These behaviors are generally very simple kinds of roles, such as going to school, going to town shopping, going to church on Sunday, going to a football game, or participating in a birthday party; but all of these roles require certain kinds of expectancies and realizations of rights and wrongs and acceptable behavior.

If a child lives upon a mountain and his father is a moonshiner and the authorities come up the mountain to arrest the father; then the rights and wrongs of this child's environment will tell him that he must p r o t e c t his father. He m u s t protect his land, his rights, his m o o n s h i n e, and consequently he will o p p o s e the legal aspects. T h e s e are the kinds of environmental influences t h a t children will b r i n g to school and then we will e x p e c t them t o change suddenly and realize t h a t our way of life is the good way of l i f e and our way of life is what is also expected of them.

Without a doubt environmental experiences prob-ably have a d e f i n i t e degree of influence u p o n a child's intellectual functioning. The c h i l d who is in a h o m e furnished with television, books, record-ings, nice Sunday dinners, outings w i t h the family, and vacations will very definitely experience a f a r wider conceptual categorization of life t h a n d o e s the c h i l d who lives in a sheltered home without the influences of television a n d books and o t h e r media of learning. T h e basic intelligence a n d potential ability for growth may l i e dormant within the child, because he has not had the o p p o r t u n i t y to expose himself t o a n experience or experiences that w i l l feed his innate ability to grow.

I think that we, teachers and p a r e n t s, should be able to indicate to children t h a t there are cer-tain expectancies of b e h a v i o r regardless of one's environmental upbringing. T h i s expectancy i s just s i m p l y a situation in which one may tell the child that i n this p a r t i c u l a r facility you do certain t h i n g s and in another f a c i l i t y you may do other things. In s c h o o l you are expected to act in cer-tain ways, and in church you a c t a c e r t a i n way. M a y b e in your home you don't act t h a t way, but in other places you will. T h i s message can be relayed

252

to the children, but it must be a message that says, "I am not forcing my way of life or society or culture upon you, but I do expect different behavior in different roles."

Sometimes it is frightening for a teacher to have a small youngster in class who is physically reactive and proficient in cursing, but you must remain aware of the fact that his environment has influenced and accepted his behavior. You, the teacher, are faced with the challenge again of creating a different environmental influence upon this child. Then, hopefully, the child will gravitate to different models of life and learn to live successfully within the world of many different environments.

FANTASY AND PLAYTIME

Play activities are extremely important to young children. Play is an expression of oneself; the kids learn some self-determination, some self- efficiency, some feeling, "I am a person, I can interact, I can do things. . ." Playtime in the fantasy world is the kids' way of escaping reality. A similar kind of escape for adults, of course, is to go fishing, go to a football game, go to a movie, or take a vacation. All of these activities are ways of escaping the frustrations of the reality world. This escape is important to life. It is good for life that we are not saddled with the day to day routine with never an escape.

The only real concern with children in the fantasy world, and it is a concern of which parents and teachers should be aware, is whether a child who is in a fantasy play can drop the role and return to the normal world. Example: A child is in the front yard playing superman, and he is superman flying around the yard enjoying himself. Mother yells, "Come to dinner, Jimmy," and the child comes into the house no longer playing superman and becomes a little boy sitting at the table eating dinner--no problem. On the other hand, we have the child who is superman in the yard and mother yells for him to come to dinner. The child flies into the kitchen and he sits down at the table and he is still superman. He is superman when he awakes. He is superman when he goes to bed. He is superman throughout the day. This kind of activity is fantasy beyond that which would be a

temporary escape from reality.   It would be a total
escape into an unreal world.   This child may need
some counseling, guidance, and evaluation.

Another aspect, which parents don't consider
about children in their play activities,   is that the
parents have a way of commanding the child immediately
to respond to parental needs.   An example would be:
Maybe this child has been out in the yard for a couple of hours playing, and he has worked all afternoon
from first base to second base to center field to
pitcher, and finally after an hour and a half or two
hours he is ready to bat; he is ready to take a swing
at the first ball.   Mother yells out the door,"You
get in here to eat immediately.   Don't delay.   I mean
right now!"   The child's whole   world has crumbled
from under him for the moment.   He worked all afternoon to have the privilege of batting the ball.   Suddenly, when he is able to do so, his fun is jerked
away from him,   and he has to drop his play world and
go to the dinner table.

Parents, most of these disappointments for the
child at play can be prevented.   I say most of them,
because you can very easily tell the child ahead of
time that you expect him home to eat at a certain
time.   You could, also, stick your head out the door
and yell at Johnny that he is to eat in 15 more minutes; therefore, he has the opportunity to get ready
to come in.   This way he knows ahead of time. He is
prepared to come to dinner.   He doesn't have to wait
until the exact moment he is going to bat the ball,
then lose his entire afternoon of play.   This advance
notice can be an effective kind of communication in
nearly all of the child's activities, because it lets

him know what you expect of him and when you expect him; rather than your pulling surprises on him just as he reaches the most important time in his play day.

GIVING - RECEIVING

Erich Fromm's book "The Art of Loving" gives a beautiful refinement of the aspects of one's giving and receiving. Fromm clearly indicates that we don't give affectively if we have a need to sacrifice ourselves; but we do give positively when in giving, we receive.

Christmas is usually a beautiful example of the great pleasure one receives from giving. So many times, though, as parents and teachers we indicate to our kids that we are giving because we believe we are the good guys. I take my son fishing and then express to him how I've given up my time and sacrificed a beautiful day at the golf c o u r s e just so I could be a good father and t a k e him fishing. This is a giving up of one's time, a sacrifice, to prove h o w great one is. It is not a t aking o f my son fishing because I receive by giving to him of my time and love. T h e boy will know. He can easily t e l l that I would rather by on the golf course than fishing with him. He will not enjoy the day, because I won't let him. I'll constantly r e m i n d h im that I'm a great father because I took him fishing.

I f you don't want to do things with or for your kids, don't do it. You'll only end up trying to convince the child of your good i n t e n t i o n s , but the child can see through the camaflouge. He knows y o u detest spending this time with him. If y o u really enjoy giving, you can't hide it. Also, if you give as a sacrifice, you can't hide it.

One summer the students from Wagon Wheel School, (private school for emotionally disturbed kids) w e r e getting r e a d y to leave the airport for their annual trip to Mexico. One of the parents walked t o their daughter and said, "I hope you will enjoy our summer vacation." In other words, "See what good parents we are, we gave up our vacation so y o u can go to Mexico. We didn't give y o u the Mexico trip because we enjoy giving to you, but instead we sacrificed ourselves for you." You can't fool these kids, parents and teachers. They know whether giving comes from the heart or the pocket book.

Do you really feel good when y o u do something nice for someone? Do you i n d i c a t e to them what a good guy you are because you give u p so much of your time, effort, and money? Examine y o u r motives for giving. Listen to y o u r comments after you've d o n e

something nice for a person. Do you like what you see
and hear?

HOMEWORK - NO!

I should like to take just a few minutes to discuss the relative merits of school homework and the
actual ramifications of this very illogical practice
which has engulfed so many teachers and parents. First,
one should examine the actual needs for homework. Careful evaluation of homework indicates to this writer
that there are very few if any constructive fulfill-
ments of the needs of students through the assignments
of page after page of homework. In most situations
homework may fulfill the needs of many teachers,
principals, and parents, but it is a terribly unjust
headache for the children. Some parents want homework
because this gets the kid out of the living room, out
from under their feet, and back into the bedroom s o
he can't be seen or heard. He can't bother anyone but
himself in the study room. If he comes out of the
study room to ask for help, the parents yell at him to
get back to his room and his homework. If he leaves
his room and does get help from mom and dad; there is
a good possibility that they may not know how to help
him; or that they may not have the patience or for-
bearance to help. Therefore, a family quarrel is
encountered and the child ends up crying and trudging

258

back toward his room, while mom and dad are yelling at each other. That is one possibility of homework! Do you like it?

Also, one must consider the hours that children spend in school. Many students--elementary and high school, small and large schools, city and farm--catch a school bus at 7:00 am and get home at 5:00 pm. This is a total of ten hours, which is a pretty long day's work. Now, add another two-three hours of homework. These children are then expected to work a total of ten-thirteen hours a day. How many hours, parents and teachers, do you spend on your job each day? If you worked 13 hours per day you probably would yell quite loudly; yet many teachers and parents expect their children in the 3rd, 4th, 5th, and high school grades to put in 13 hours a day. Does this really make sense?

I firmly believe that little kids need a lot of physical activity each day. It is quite impossible to have children involved in play activities if they are controlled by school work for 10-13 hours each day.

Consider another very important aspect of homework--concepts of the assigned task. Why, teacher, do you send work home with the child? Can you really answer that question? If a teacher sends home 40 arithmetic problems to a 5th grade student, and the student has the concept of what he should do; he would have repetition of tasks that would be of little conceptual or categorical value. Another child may have no concept of the task at hand, so he takes homework home and can't work the problems. Dad can't help. Mother can't help. What has been accomplished?

Some other kids take work h o m e and the parents complete the assignment for the children and send them back to school with great expectations of getting all A's on their report card.

Another point for consideration should be for the student's home environment. Too many variables exist within the students environment which prevent the <u>justification</u> of homework. Some youngsters have paper routes and need to go to bed early. Some students have many chores to do at home--dishes, b a b y-sitting, and outside jobs. Some children may have to attend church three-four nights a week. Are we to punish these young people for attending church? Homework surely does. Some pupils have plenty of f r e e time to do homework, a n d parents who may help them or even do the homework for them.

Look very carefully at the highly motivated and hard working student. He does very well on his homework assignment. Tomorrow he takes it back to class and the teacher skims over the assignment. The child responds, "I worked hard and the teacher didn't even take a grade." On another day the student is unable to do his h o m e w o r k and this is the day the teacher really evaluates his assignment and g i v e s a grade. He then has an "F" for that assignment. Is homework really fair? There is only one answer--"No," and we wonder why kids l e a r n to h ate teachers, parents, and school.

Homework or busywork is our concern. I am not advocating a total abandonment of homework. Yes, I do realize that there are scattered t i m e s w h e n a teacher must send work home with t h e s t u d e n t s because there are t i m e s when students will work on special projects and need to do homework which is justified. There is a great concern, though, with the teacher who consistently assigns homework when the only visible objective in most s i t u a t i o n s is one which says, "Teachers must give homework." Most teachers r e a l l y have no objective or goal for homework other than the p r e s s u r e s that they feel from themselves, parents, and principals. This pressure is the result of many years o f traditionally pseudo concepts that supposedly constitute a good teacher. If the t e a c h e r s do not pile on the work, they are threatened by some pseudo rational that says they are not good teachers.

If you, the teacher or principal, get pressure from parents; e x p l a i n to them that you do not believe in consistent homework and that children taught well in school are much better students than children who are c o n f u s e d with homework assignments. If a teacher spends the time wisely during the school day, the child should have sufficient opportunity to work and to achieve for one day. Many times, though, teachers w i l l spend 40 minutes of the hour talking and talking and talking; and the kids are mumbling to themselves; "Gaw, I wish she'd shutup and let us get to work." Finally the teacher will quit talking and say, "Hurry up now, get your assignment finished, you have only ten minutes to finish or you'll h a v e to take your work home with you." Therefore, the continuation of the vicious cycle of the homework evil.

Teachers and parents, before you reject the statements of this article, hesitate a few moments and really reflect upon your experience with chil-

dren and your consistent battles with homework. These
reflections won't present a very pleasant picture,
I'm sure; and at this time there appears to be no
particular way of establishing a homework program
that is compatible with the needs of the majority
of the students, parents, and teachers. Therefore,
it appears to be much more sensible to reduce, reduce,
and reduce the amount of homework.

Do you ever stop to realize how e f f e c t i v e it is when you receive a n immediate reward for some-thing that is of value to you? For example: you come into the house w i t h a new hair-do, a nice new dress, or something which affectively should make you feel well. As you walk through the door you get a response from those around you, a message that says, "That is a beautiful dress." "Your hair really looks sharp." "You really look great today." You have an immediate reward. You feel great. There is't a straining affect.

Now you walk through the door and you have a new dress or a nice hair-do, but nobody responds. You wait an hour. You wait two hours. You're around the house. Maybe you eat dinner. Eventually, somebody says, "Hummm, got a new hair-style today, huh?" How did you finally feel? Probably not very darn good. The total e f f e c t o f the immediate affect is gone. You needed a compliment when you walked in the door. You needed help when the hair-style was new; when it was immediate to you, not an hour later, not two hours later; not at somebody's convenience.

Parents, teachers, if you receive a response from a child, a task well done; immediately r e w a r d the child for his efforts. You don't have to wait until school is out. You don't have to wait until next Sunday, next Saturday, or whenever it is convenient for you to r e w a r d a child. If a child has done a good job on some task, right then and there is when he needs to be rewarded for that task. If you wait until school is out and he is on his way home and say, "You did a good job today, Johnny." That doesn't have nearly the effect upon the child as it would if you rewarded him after his immeidate accomplishment of the task.

As a parent you are having problems (as an example) with your child at the dinner table. The child is perhaps slopping around the table in an unfit kind of way. If you want to change this child's behavior you're probably going to accomplish far more if you make some rewarding c o m p l i m e n t a number of times throughout the meal when he does something well; rather t h a n waiting until the meal is over and then respond by saying, "Well, you did pretty well today, Johnny, maybe tomorrow you can do a little better." Success breeds success; there is no way in the world it can be any other way. If a child responds well at the dinner table, you should reward him immediately for doing well and then c o n t i n u e to reward him for his total effort. We learn to accept rewards by teaching children to never defense out or excuse compliments. We, adults, even refuse compliments by making e x c u s e s for our good behavior or dress. If someone rewards you with a compliment; accept it with confidence. If someone says to you, "Gee, you look great." Respond with a simple, "Thank you, I feel great."

G e n e r a l l y, a compliment is given because the person really means what he says ; yet many people continually excuse thenselves when they are complimen t e d because they feel that they must earn the compliment or e l s e they become suspicious of one's complimenting motives, "What does he want? He's up to something fishy." What your're saying, is that you don't deserve to hear good about yourself. The converse of this, parents and teachers, is when a child compliments you. He probably believes his compliment. He's not purely manipulating. Therefore, you should say something nice back to him immediately, and believe me, it will make for a heck-of-a-lot nicer child.

It's not knowing the consequences of one's actions that causes considerable discomfort. If a child is somewhat aware of his rewards for good behavior and the consequences for poor behavior; he will not feel tricked, cheated, or learn to mistrust the adults. Many times we determine the consequence that we plan to administer, but we have delays in our implementation, which in effect releases the order and the child believes he is no longer under that obligation. Sometimes as parents, punishment or consequences are placed on a time basis and the punishment has no relationship to the severity of the problem. Let me point out the inconsistency; for example, as a parent you ground your child for three weeks. There is a possibility that in this three weeks' period there are no activities which the child will miss. Therefore, his is losing nothing. He has three weeks at home, no big deal. Another month he is grounded for the same period of three weeks; but during this three weeks' period the student misses the school play, the spring prom, a ball game, or a number of other school activities. Consequently, this three weeks' period results in excessive consequences. Therefore, relate the severity of his actions to the values associated with the things that the child is being denied.

We seem constantly to tell our kids that they must be individuals. Yet when the kids do withdraw into themselves and exclude the group, we become concerned because they don't interact with other people. Surely, we must help the kids to help themselves , but there really is no way we can become totally individualistic and function adequately in this old world. We need other people. We have to have other people before we can make it. There just is no way that one can compatibly live in this world by being a total individual. Each day we must play a different role. In fact we may have to perform many different roles each day. We perform in school, at home, at church, in a movie, or at a ball game; and each place will constitute a modification of one's behavior.

If one were to become very individualistic, he probably would become quite suspicious of other people. We have to depend on others, and if one is too afraid of others, he may be unable to make friends. He will not trust a person enough to allow a close relationship.

Whenever you see a group process working well-- kids at play, a basketball or football team, a minister and his Sunday attendance, a large industrial firm, the U. S. Army, or any other group --you'll realize that there is a mutual goal for all the people in the group. When one person loses sight of this mutual goal and decides that he wishes to be an individual and that he doesn't need anyone else, the mutual goal, or objective, is lost and there is a breaking down of the group.

Essentially this is one of the processes applied to Korean POW's. In World War II if a POW were to try for an escape, he could depend upon help from the group. They had a mutual goal. In Korea, the POW's were suspicious and afraid that their buddies would turn them in if one said, "Let's escape." There was no mutual goal; these persons were brainwashed to individualism--you can't depend on anyone, no one will help you.

Let me show you another example. About four years ago we decided to take the six most disturbed kids from Wagon Wheel School, (Mc Loud , Oklahoma, a private school for emotionally disturbed kids) and put them in a summer p r o g r a m with a man and woman counselor to work on a group process. Whatever happened at the camp was to be determined by the group. If one boy had a problem be could call a group meeting and depend on the others. Each boy could call a group meeting on another student, on the counselor, or on the psychological consultants. Consequently, it was to be a group process, no one was to be alone or handle his problems alone. (If you notice kids who are having problems, one of the typical responses will be, "Leave me alone, I don't need anybody else. I can handle my own problems." That should be evidence enough to indicate that he can't handle his own problems.)

Anyhow, this group of six boys and two counselors built a cabin for the summer and started working on a large cabin. We told them they had to work at least four hours each day, and the rest of the time could be spent freely--fishing, hiking, etc. As the days passed, we noticed that there was very little progress. A group meeting was called and the boys told us that they would work four hours and build the building, but they wanted to set their own schedule. We agreed, because we were interested in the mutual goals. These boys had wild schedules. They may work from 12:00 am to 4:00 pm, or from 8:00 pm to 12:00 midnight; but they did work, and the finished product was a beautiful, two-story, A-frame building with kitchen, bath, bedrooms, and lounge.

As September rolled along, the boys all enrolled in a neighboring rural school. Some comments, "Boy, I like school." "For the first time school is OK," indicated somewhat that the mutuality of the group had a carryover effect to school. School continued for a few months successfully and the boys would call their group meetings, talk out their problems, and maintain a dependence on each other and the Mr. and Mrs. Counselors. We suddenly lost our Mr. and Mrs. Counselors and we replaced them with two inexperienced people, a man and a woman. These two counselors did not follow through with the group meetings, nor did they project the accepting mother-father roles that we felt were so necessary. The mutual goals started breaking down. The kids didn't need each other anymore. They became total individuals and started fighting and fussing with eachother. Their dependency on help from one's fellow man dissolved. One day they left for public school and after a couple of hours at school they all skipped-out and walked back to the camp site. The counselors had gone to do the grocery shopping; and the kids, left alone, proceeded to destroy the building. They knocked out all the windows, ripped up the furniture and bed upholstery, tore off the refrigerator door, broke the bathroom sink and commode from their connections, and in general really destroyed the place. We sent two home, two to mental hospitals, and kept two. The point is that we must have need for our fellow man. We need others and others need us. We must have common or mutual goals in life, because there is no way to make it alone in this world.

I have known principals who have built pride, es spirit de corps, in their schools by continually allowing the kids to feel that the school was theirs and that the school served their needs; consequently, vandalism was almost nil because the kids wouldn't destroy what was theirs. It is singularly and mutually mine, and I'm proud of my school, my home, my brother and sister, my mother and father, my cat, or whatever may be of mutual concern.

Marriages are dissolved when we lose sight of our mutual goals. When husbands and wives have mine and yours, they no longer need each other. They are competitors. I have my money; you have yours, and somebody always loses. When you compete for goals rather than having mutual goals; somebody loses and somebody wins. He who is losing will try harder to win and destroy the other person. We need each other. You are not a teacher without the kids. You are not a teacher if the kids don't learn. You are not a parent without kids. You do not have a marriage, a home, a family without mutual goals and needs and understanding for each other. Don't compete with your wife, your husband, your children, your school. Share with each other and reach for that which involves each of you in a compatible, not competitive way.

LIKE-DISLIKE

As teachers and parents we may be much more effective in our roles if we recognize our likes and dislikes for different children. Typically, parents and teachers respond that they treat all their children the same fair way, which is impossible. The teacher and parent can only imply that equal treatment is pledged to all kids. Ask the students and see if they respond that they receive equally fair treatment. These kids can very quickly point out the children who receive or don't receive the proper attention from parents and teachers.

Each child will get feedback from the expression of the adult in different ways. For example, there are many ways one can say, "I love you." These three words may have a tone and expression which indicate love, amusement, satire, hate, happiness, loneliness, or fear. The words alone do not constitute a message, but the mood and expressions through one's actions tell the true story.

An old dumb dog doesn't understand the words, "I love you," but this dog will recognize when someone likes or dislikes him. Needless to say, if a dog can receive a like or dislike message, it is quite certain that we can't fool a child.

Your actions, teachers and parents, tell the child what one really feels. Words are only surface varifications of love and affection. True warmth must be conveyed if love is to be meaningful. Love is an experience that is essential to one's ability to give and receive.

Therefore, my suggestion is that we should try to recognize our likes and dislikes. If you can't stand a child, confess this to yourself and you will probably be able to treat the child fairly. You may not like a person, but you can be honest and fair with him. We have ways of setting our limits and understanding our feelings, but we can't set limits if we don't acknowledge how we really feel.

If one knows a person and knows that each likes the other; one can set his limits and get along quite well. If one does not like a person, and recognizes that both dislike each other, again limits are set and each will go his way; in this manner they too have found a way to get along with each other. It's the person in the middle who is uncomfortable. He doesn't know whether he's liked or disliked. If a child sits in a classroom day in and day out, not knowing whether the teacher likes him or dislikes him; he will constantly be trying to realize where he stands. Even if he knows the teacher doesn't like him, he will be more comfortable than if he were constantly vascillating back and forth.

Now I am not saying that we as parents and teachers, should yell out to our kids that we dislike them, "Hey, kid, I can't stand you." I am saying that we should not try to convince them that we really like them when in reality we can't stand the little squirts. If you can become aware of your likes and dislikes, then by being realistic, you can have a much better relationship with your children.

Remember, you should not verbally say to a child, "I hate you;" nor should you try to make him believe that you love him when you don't. Just be honest with yourself and the child. He will then know where he stands; and both you and the child will be more comfortable.

MOTIVATION

Motivation is a word that has been completely worn out by educators, parents, individualists, and the productive areas of life and work. It is quite difficult to get a person to realize a good concept of motivation. I don't really know what motivation is. I think I know what it isn't, therefore, I have some assumptions upon which to offer suggestions. Our school principals say that the teacher should motivate those kids. College professors say we should motivate college students. Parents expect teachers to motivate their students, but we never seem to learn just how this can be accomplished. Motivation is not what we have to offer a child. Motivation is the within factor. It must come from within the person. The student must have sincere need and desire to excell before he will succeed. Naturally, the concept of one's self again enters into the picture, and adults stimulate the children to form concepts of themselves; but we do not motivate children. As adults, teachers, we can only offer a child that which we have, experience, education, empathy to their feelings, and our time. If the child does not respond, teachers should not become personally involved in a win or lose situation; because with some kids one will win and succeed, and with others one will fail.

If the teacher has thirty to thirty-five children in a class, expectations of success for all children would, at times, be unrealistic. Some children will not respond to the teacher's stimuli. This is not to say that the teacher should become complacent and give up. Surely the teacher will respond to the challenge and continue to search for the material and emotional stimuli to which the child will respond. Yet teachers should not be self-condemning when frustrations and failure appear in the classroom. Some children are seemingly without motivational values, and any person who has had an unresponsive child in a classroom will be aware of the cold unaffected kinds of feedback that this child exudes.

Therefore, teachers, express yourselves professionally to the highest degree by giving of yourself, your time, your education, your experience, your emotions, and your intellect; and if the child does not respond, try again; but do not continue to punish yourself for inadequacy. Other people have probably also failed in their efforts to provide stimulation for this child, and as a parent or teacher you can never know what exactly may stimulate a child. We do know, however, that motivation is a within factor. It must come from within the child, and you cannot give that motivation to the child. Therefore, we must continue to offer avenues of stimulation that will hopefully activate his inner motivations which in turn will enable the child to realize the progress and the accomplishment of tasks and roles of life that will be compatible for his well-being.

PARENT-TEACHER CONFERENCE

There are some procedures or techniques within the parent teacher conferencing situation that I feel may be of value to both parents and teachers. First it appears to be quite essential that the parent and the teacher both greet each other in a warm, somewhat pleasant way. I don't feel that either the parent or the teacher will benefit at all from a situation that starts off on a complaining, grouching, unhappy kind of note. I am sure that the parent and teacher, both, will be observing each other and watching feedback that exists between the two. Feedback which is obvious when the teacher becomes defensive about her work, and when the parent starts blaming the teacher for the child's inability to have learned that which they feel is essential for the school year.

It is very important that both the parent and the teacher be frank and honest with each other. If the teacher discusses realistically, the progress that the child is making, then I am sure that the parent probably will in most cases be in agreement, because they probably have observed the same things. I think that the worst thing that a teacher can do to the parent; and probably the last thing the parent wants, is for the teacher to neglect problems that the child is having today and give the parents false hope with such comments as, "Your child will grow out of it; it is only a phase." "The child will make it next year." "Don't worry, the child will work through it." This is an easy way the teacher can get off the hook, and project potentially serious educational problems onto next year's teacher.

I should suggest to the teacher that if you have realistic ways in which you can ask the parents to help the child's educational program, then do so; but I do believe, and quite strongly, that you should not suggest to the parent to help the child just for the sake of helping the child. If you don't have a particular purpose or reason for the parent to work with the child at home, then don't suggest such things. I repeat, I am totally against the traditional concept of homework, which is something that is going to cause more problems in the home.

It is wise, extremely wise, for the teacher to avoid any language around the parent that indicates a labeling of the child. Many times we can make comments about the child in which we have very subtle, indirect implications that say to the parent, "He's a dumb kid." "He's an idiot." "He's a trouble maker."

Of course, this message will only upset the parents that much more, and they will go away from the conference feeling badly, and then they will resentfully indicate to their neighbors and friends that the teacher called my kid stupid, trouble maker, etc. So be careful, very careful, with the comments that you make about the child to the parent. Any labeling will probably be a false labeling, and it will be one which will only create more problems.

I think it is extremely important to try to maintain a confidence level with parents. Many parents have a very negative feeling toward teachers and schools at the present time; thus if the parents come to a conference and are confronted with a rigid, complaining, grouchy, incompatible appearing teacher, they very quickly will lose what little confidence they may have had in the school system. Therefore, try to maintain confidence, try to appear to the parent that you are aware of what is going on, and that you have no reason to be defensive; that you don't have to hop in and explain to the parent all the reasons that would justify everything that you are doing. Instead try to maintain an image that says that you know what you are doing and what you are doing is the proper way of teaching.

The conference can provide a defensive situation for both parents and teachers. The parent will ask a teacher why his Johnny can't read, and the teacher will then respond defensively for his teaching techniques, which will convey a message that says, "If the kid doesn't learn it's not my fault, because I have taught properly; you just have a stupid kid." Rather than defend your teaching techniques, I believe you can reach a much more compatible understanding of the child's problems if you return to the parents the same question, "Why do you think Johnny can't read?" You may be surprised by the response you will get from the parents. They may tell you things about the child that exist within the home that would be of value to you as his teacher. Things that may open a door to Johnny and allow him to move through and become a reading student rather than a non-reading student. Again, it is extremely important that you don't get into a defensive war with each other, but instead compliment each other; with a positive attitude you are more likely to have a workable situation.

Finally, try to end the conference on a pleasant note. It will be of great advantage to both parents and teachers, if the conversation closes with a complimentary and trusting exchange of intellect and affect.

PUNISHMENT-RELATED TO OFFENSE

I think many times that as parents and teachers we become extremely punitive. By punitive I mean we are punishing people. We are inconsistent in our administration of punishment. One time, as a parent or teacher, we may let a child get by with something. The next day we will give him a 500 word theme to write, as punishment. The next day we will kick him out of class. The next day we will send him to the principal's office. The next day we will give him a spanking--and on and on.

Now, I know that it can be extremely difficult to relate the offense to the punishment--consequence. By this I mean, if a child does something wrong in the classroom or at home, try relating the punishment to this particular offense. An example would be: if the child is acting out at the dinner table, the punish - ment should then pertain to the dinner time activity. Maybe the logical thing here would be to dismiss the child from the dinner table.

Wagon Wheel School has a policy under which they function with their emotionally disturbed children, that says; if, in the evening, a child acts out in the kitchen then he is dismissed from the kitchen. He is not denied other privileges. If he goes to a movie on Saturday night and he acts out in the movie, then he loses that privilege. If he is misbehaving during horseback riding, he loses that privilege. If he mis- behaves in other situations he will lose those partic- ular privileges; he will not lose all other privileges for having misbehaved in only one activity. In this way the child can understand the relationship between his inappropriate actions and the activities which are denied him.

I think, also, that we should try letting them know ahead of time what the consequences may be. There is a difference, I think, between punishment and con- sequences. Punishment usually means something that is done impromptly or impulsively. We immediately jump on the kid's action and administer punishment that says, "This is a result of what you have done."

"This is what you are going to get, you little so and so." And then we dish out, then and there, what we feel may be justified for what the child has done. A consequence would be involved when the child is aware ahead of time, "If I do a certain thing then this will be the result of that action." An example would be: If you were driving down a highway and saw a stop sign at the intersection. You neglected to stop. At that time a policeman pulls up and he says, "I think maybe I will fine you $50.00 today." You would be far more uncomfortable in that situation not knowing what the punishment would be. However, your anxiety would be considerably diminished if you knew the consequences; it would be more comfortable to know that if you run a stop sign there would be a specific fine of $20.00, rather than the uncertain amount arbitrarily decided upon by the partolman at that moment.

We should stabilize the consequences with kids ahead of time; then as parents and teachers, we should follow through with the consequences. Set up the consequences as contingent upon certain behavior; then do it. Don't wait until the child's activity level is visible and then release the order and let him get by with it. Example: Many times parents use, as I mentioned previously, the typical grounding situation. In this instance the child performs in an unacceptable manner and is grounded for three weeks. Now this may be good; it may not be good. But let me point out how inconsistently this grounding does not relate punishment to misbehavior. For three weeks the child may sit at home and miss nothing; hence there would be very little punishment. Another three weeks could involve missing a big athletic program, the Christmas dance, the school play, etc. There are a number of things that could happen in a three week period. I could see one three week period when a child may not be denied any privileges, and I could see another three week period in which a child may be denied many privileges. That is why I feel that you should, if possible, administer the punishment and relate it to the disobedience or misbehavior. I think it is important, parents and teachers, for you to realize what the child is denied; to see what you are doing to him before you yell out, "You are......" and then name a punishment. Whatever kind of punishment you use, will be of no value at all unless there is a misbehavior relationship. Punishment r e l a t e d to misbehavior tells the child that there is acceptance between parent and child, and teacher and child; this in turn encourages an understanding which says, "I am being punished because of what I did, not because of what I am."

REACTING TO ACTIONS, NOT WORDS

I think there is a certain kind of intangible need within some people that says to children, "Here I am, and you'd better behave." On the other hand, I think there is certain feedback from some adults that says, "Here I am kid, you can get by with anything." I think the thing that happens is that too often we give a command in a way that is hesitant, without confidence; and many times the child accurately interprets the message as saying, "He doesn't really mean what he says; he isn't really going to do what he says." Thus, it is useless, totally useless, for us as parents and teachers, to command a child to do something and then release the command and never follow through. There seems to be an interesting kind of phenomena relative to parents or teachers giving orders to children. Precisely, this is a situation in which parents feel that after they give a command to a child, there should be an automatic response to that command. Those of us who have been around children for any period of time realize that this is a false assumption.

Before a child will react to a verbal command, there must be some association of action with words. By this I mean that one has to have significant authority attached to the command that says to the child, "You will do whatever the request or command requires." An example would be that if you as a parent or teacher tell a child to do something, then you should be sure that you can follow through. A child will react to your actions, not to what you say. You may have a child in your classroom to whom you say, "Johnny, sit down. Johnny, this is the last time, sit down. Johnny, I'm not going to tell you again; sit down." This goes on for 15 or 20 minutes or perhaps the whole hour. Long before the hour is over Johnny knows that you are not going to make him sit in his chair, or any where else. Consequently, he shows no reaction to your words, because there are no actions from you to support your own command. The result of this situation is that Johnny will not only continue his out-of-seat behavior, he will continue to ignore your commands now and in the future.

If you the parent or teacher will commit yourself to follow through with your command, the child will soon learn to react to your words as well as to your actions. Then, when you say, "Johnny, sit down," he will sit down. Although there is sound reasoning to support the use of this method and the end result is beneficial to all concerned; the initial task which requires consistency in following through, often needs more time than some of us are willing to give. Many times as parents and teachers we use our inconsistent methods, with their inconsistent results, as a means of justifying our spanking the child. For example, the parent who tells the child, "Stop yelling. Go to your room. Go to your room and go to bed. Get out of my sight, I can't stand all your noise." This is repeated many times and the child sits in the middle of the floor still making noise and messing with the toy. Finally mother or father gets up and just clobbers the daylights out of the kid. The response is, "It's all your fault kid. I told you, and told you, and you're still making noise. Now you're going to get it. You asked for it. It's not my fault. I don't feel any guilt about punishing you, because you had your opportunity and you didn't mind me."

This nonsense can be avoided. Follow through at once with your command. Do not release it. Keep the command active until the task is complete. An example would be a parent or teacher who gives a command to a child, "It's time to go to bed; go get ready for bed." The child continues to play and the parent again commands, "Go to bed." This verbal process continues for a number of minutes, maybe even an hour; finally the parent says, "OK, for the last time, I've told you to go to bed, now go to bed." And the parent jumps up, grabs the child, rushes him down the hall to the bedroom. The child finally has received a message, but he is probably confused. The parent has probably realized some justification for his having hit the child or whatever action he has taken, by blaming the lack of response to the parent's command.

The evidence, of course, is that the child will continue to play in the middle of the room. He will continue to do whatever he is doing until he relates some meaning to the command and the actions from the teacher or the parent.

I believe it is far better as a teacher or parent not to make any kind of a command to a child if you are unable to follow through with the action. Therefore, if you're going to make a command and release it by not following through, then make it again only to release it, ultimately there will be no meaning attached to what you tell the child. It will then be pointless to make any suggestion that the child perform in a given manner or complete a specific task.

It is really an easily activated situation for a parent to put actions and words together by simply saying to the child, "It is time to go to bed," then immediately if the child doesn't respond; the parent should get up from that comfortable chair, walk over to the child, pick him up, usher him with some physical authority to the bedroom. Let him know this is a command to be obeyed. After this procedure has been implemented a few times, the child will get a message that says, "My dad said to go to bed, and my dad's actions indicate that he wants me to go to bed, which means I had better start moving."

I think sometimes as parents and teachers we excuse out vindictive actions toward an unresponsive child, when realistically we could have saved ourselves a lot of trouble and the child a lot of punishment had we simply followed through with the command the first time we gave it.

The following is a personal example I witnessed of parent-verbal-command to a child. The parent drove her car up to the front of the clinic, got out of the car, walked around the car, and opened the door for the child to get out. The child slid across to the other side of the car. The parent walked around the car and opened the other door, and the child slid back to the other side. The parent walked back around to the other side of the car and the child slid back to the other side. This procedure of walking back and forth around the car, opening the door, and the child sliding back and forth happened about 12-15 times, Finally, the parent reached into the car, pulled the kid out of the car onto the sidewalk and just beat the daylights out of him. The parent was saying to the child, "You had 15 chances to get out of the car and you didn't do it; now I'm going to beat the heck out of you." Therefore, the parent's rational is "Child, it is your fault that you are getting this beating."

Again, it is very simple to see that the first time the parent opened the door and told the child to get out and come into the office was the time to reach into the car, pull the child out, and gently walk him to the clinic. I think sometimes we may need to examine how much we need the kids to punish us. Are we going to let this kind of thing go and go, until we really punish ourselves because we have to punish the kids?

We really aren't dealing with a very difficult situation when we need to follow through on our commands. It is a simple matter of saying something to your child then reacting physically to back up what you have said. Make sure you do not release a command and be sure that the child does as you have told him. If you can't follow through with your commands, then please don't give the orders. If you give an order and release the child from obeying; then very simply the child has won, and you as a parent or teacher, have lost.

SCHOOL GRADES A-F's

As a parent or teacher have you ever asked yourself the question, "What is my concept of grading? What is my concept of school grades?" We should take a good look at this grading scale: A, B, C, D, and F. Just what exactly does it mean? What does it communicate to us when a child gets an A, a B, a C, a D, or an F? Probably the first thing we indicate with this grading scale is that the child is failing. Even though he has received an A and maybe a B, a couple of C's and one F, that means he is failing. This is not a concept of the total program, this is a concept of total failure. The child received an F in one subject, an A, a B, and a couple of C's in other subjects; now let's face it, that really isn't a terrible average.

You put all of these grades together and the child isn't doing too badly, but the chances are if that child takes that report card to the parents, they will not see the A; they will not see the B, the C's; they will see one thing, that's the F. Immediate response to this will be, "Why, why did you make an F?" There will be no attention given to the A, to the B, to the C's, but all the attention will be given to the F.

Next report card comes home and the child has one A, one B, one C, and two F's. Again, all of the attention is given to the F's. The child will direct his efforts to the attention he gets from the F's. You direct your concern and attention as a parent or teacher to the F's, and to this attention the child will gravitate.

Really now, wouldn't it be much easier to look at the child's report card and compliment the A, compliment the B, and somewhat ignore the F's. Now I am not saying totally ignore the F; what I am saying is, don't attend to it exclusively; give a reward, a reinforcement to the A's, the B's. Give the child a chance to gravitate to the rewards of good grades, not to your attention to the F's.

I'm not going to get into the value or the merits of the A, B, C, D, F system; because it appears we are somewhat stuck with this system of grading and at the present time there doesn't appear to be anything that works any more compatibly in the school system than the A's, B's, C's, D's, and F's. The fact remains, though, there are a mumber of ways that we can treat and respond to these particular grades or this grading system. I have just indicated that by attending to the good rather than attending to the bad, should in effect help get the kinds of results that most parents desire of their children on report cards.

STRUCTURE

Structure is an extremely important aspect of life in that it benefits both children and adults. There is no way in the world that we can live compatibly if we don't have limited structures placed upon us. If you were to pull up to a corner and there were no stop lights or signs, you would be much more uncomfortable than if you have the structure of a stop light or stop sign. Someone or something telling you, that you must obey, that you must do this, that there are rules and regulations, is comforting. If we are left to decide for ourselves all of the things that we may choose to do, we would be spending all of our time trying to decide what we should or should not do. It is much easier for us to live in a world in which things are somewhat predetermined.

A freshman girl who lives in a college dorm is

a much more confident girl living in the dorm with someone telling her she must be in by nine o'clock You can only stay out until a certain hour on Saturdays and Sundays. You cannot have boys in your room. You must go to bed at a certain time. These are all things that are decided for her. She doesn't have to decide. This responsibility is taken off her shoulders. She doesn't have to decide each night what time she will come in, and what time she will get up, or what time she will eat. I am sure this young lady is more comfortable than she would be without the rules and regulations that are placed upon her.

Watch ten or twelve young kids playing in your front yard sometime. You first look out, and they are gathered into a group of unorganized youngsters. They are running and yelling, and they don't know what is going on. Walk away and come back a half hour or an hour later. Usually you will see organization when you come back; the kids will have organized. They have a game going on; there are leaders; there are followers, there are certain rules under which they must play. This is structure. Without it a kid is very uncomfortable.

Now, I'm not saying that we should structure the child's life to the point that he becomes dependent. But I am saying that we should give him guidelines, not do everything for him; but set limits for him.

I have seen a number of these boys, teenage boys, with whom I have worked in a private school for emotionally disturbed children who have been enrolled because they have deviated somewhat from society. They have had trouble at school, with parents, with church. They have grown long hair. They have begun the "hippie-kind" of syndrome. We have a rule which structurally says you cannot grow your hair lower than your eyebrows. It cannot extend lower than the top of the ear. It cannot be lower than the collar on your shirt. Time and again I have seen these boys respond, "I don't want my hair cut. I won't have it cut. I can't function without long hair and you can't make me cut it." The hair is cut and invariably these boys will come back with statements such as, "Gosh I'm glad someone made me cut my hair. I really didn't like it long, but I couldn't make myself cut it. I'm glad someone made me do it." This is structure consistency.

A friend of mine had a young boy who had a short hair cut, and over the summer the boy let his hair grow long. When school started he asked his dad, "Shall I leave my hair long or should I have it cut short again?" His dad responded, "It's your hair. Why don't you make up your mind how you want it?" His father told me that this boy walked around for a couple of weeks in a real state of anxiousness trying to decide what to do with his hair. He couldn't decide whether to cut it short, or leave it long. Again, In this situation structure was needed. This boy would have been comfortable had his dad said, "Cut it," or "Leave it long." Either way , had structure been made available, the boy would have felt more at ease.

The extreme of this would be the parent who has put so much structure into the child's life that he cannot function properly with himself. I worked with a mother who had two boys, age twelve and ten, with IQ's of 150 and 160 respectively. Neither of these children could read. The mother had "mothered" them to the point that they were totally dependent upon her for everything they did. They could not do any-thing unless she showed them how. They went down to the creek one cold winter day and came back home wet and frozen. The mother said, "Why did you do it?" The boys responded, "You didn't tell us not to." This is the way they functioned. They couldn't think for themselves. This is not structure. This is "smother-ing." This is overprotecting. This is caring for the child so much that he cannot care for himself. I do not mean to stress this kind of structure. There is a great difference between structuring a child's life, and immobilizing a child's life by commanding or doing for him.

TEACHERS & PARENTS HATE KIDS

We must realize that all people cannot be the best in their professions. We have good and bad doctors, lawyers, engineers, teachers, and parents.

Socially one must believe that teachers and parents love kids. That is the reason they give of themselves to the profession and parenthood. Although just being a parent or teacher does not automatically make one effective, affective, and accepting of his role.

If one were unconsciously to hate kids, where could he find a better place to hate, pick on, disturb, punish, make it rough on these kids. A teacher would have a captive audience--thirty kids to hate in one group.

Have you ever heard a teacher give it the ole Will Rogers try? "I just love all my children; there is never a child I don't love." For some teacher this may be a possibility. For others, however, it is a surface circuiting of their defenses for hating these kids. These adults are trying to convince themselves that they love children. One who really consciously and unconsciously loves will not have to verbalize this creed to all who are within listening distance. Instead, this person will perform as one who loves, not talk as one who must convince his group of how nice a person he is.

Let's face facts, it is nearly impossible to have thirty to thirty-five kids in a classroom year after year and love all of those little darlings. Some of these kids will bug the daylights out of a teacher and the teacher will despise them. There is then, no better way to get even than to camouflage love for the child and plan a sneak attack to destroy. Yes, I agree, this teacher or parent may consciously believe they love these kids, but unconsciously they can't stand them.

We should be able to recognize that there will be days as parents and teachers that we feel like murdering those little demons, but we won't. However, we should be able to accept those feelings without being threatened and without magnifying our feelings of guilt totally out of proportion.

Again, all parents and teachers cannot love all their children equally, if at all; therefore, try to recognize the symptoms of pain when you feel anger toward a child; and then don't camouflage your feelings. Face yourself and realize that this is the way you feel. You will live through the day and you will not surface conditions upon these children which may help destroy their personal growth and adjustment.